Music for the Mass 2
Choir edition (full music)
Including music for Holy Week and Easter, and for Weddings and Funerals

Edited by Geoffrey Boulton Smith
and Christopher McCurry

GEOFFREY
CHAPMAN

Geoffrey Chapman
A Cassell imprint
Villiers House, 41–47 Strand, London WC2N 5JE
387 Park Avenue South, New York, NY 10016-8810

Compilation and editorial material © Geoffrey Chapman, a Cassell imprint, 1993

First published 1993

British Library Cataloguing-in-Publication Data
A catalogue record for this book is available from the British Library.

Library of Congress Cataloging-in-Publication Data
Applied for.

ISBN 0-225-66659-6

Music and text typeset by Linda Lancaster Music Setting, Huddersfield
Printed and bound in Malta by Interprint Limited

Contents

Introduction: the arrangement of the book and how to use it

Music for the Mass 2 follows the general principles governing the choice and arrangement of material of *Music for the Mass 1*, but with certain important modifications to ensure greater clarity and assist a more thoughtful approach to musical decisions within the liturgy. Since Vatican II, a form of Sung Mass in which choices are made and not everything is sung has become increasingly the norm in parishes. The arrangement and contents of *Music for the Mass 2* aim to facilitate this and to reflect the priorities that need to be considered. Thus no complete settings of the Mass are included as such, but music for the different parts of the Mass—Penitential Rite, Glory to God, Gospel Acclamation, Eucharistic Acclamations (Holy, holy, Memorial Acclamation, Amen)— is grouped together so that those responsible for parish music can decide first what parts of the Mass are to be sung and then choose appropriate settings.

There are also sections for Entrance/Gathering, Preparation of the Gifts, Communion and Recession. Choices, however, should not be restricted to these sections, since at the end of the book there is a section of Songs for Various Occasions where songs that might be equally suitable for different uses have been placed. Thus Graham Kendrick's *Shine, Jesus, shine* (277) could make an equally good Entrance or Recessional song, or Jacques Berthier's *The Lord is my light* (268) might be very appropriate for communion.

For the Rite of Communion there are two sections, Breaking of Bread/Communion and Communion Songs. The former includes not only shorter settings of the Lamb of God, to accompany the fraction, but longer songs designed to begin with the fraction and to continue during the reception of communion. The latter contains songs simply to accompany the reception of communion.

In the Holy Week and Easter section we have attempted to provide for all the texts that should be sung, including all the psalms at the Easter Vigil. These psalms have been kept very simple; those looking for a more varied diet will find this in other collections specifically devoted to the psalms. For weddings we include two particularly appropriate psalms and an Alleluia as well as several hymns and songs. The funeral music can be used fairly flexibly.

Apart from the psalms mentioned in the preceding paragraph there is not room in this book to include specific Responsorial Psalms for the Sundays of the year. However, many of the texts set to music are psalm-based and some of these could be used as the Responsorial Psalm at Mass.

The numbering of the songs, starting at 153, follows on directly from *Music for the Mass 1*. Where settings include sections for Cantor/Choir and for the people, lower case letters are used for the former and capitals for the latter. Where songs are sung either by the Cantor/Choir alone or by all throughout, lower case lettering is used. The term Cantor/Choir should be interpreted liberally, depending on the resources available. Finally, a large proportion of the music includes guitar chords as well as keyboard accompaniment to facilitate variety in supporting the singing, and sometimes additional instrumental parts.

Part I · Introductory Rites

I · 1 Entrance/Gathering Songs

153 Prepare the way (Luke 3:4 & 6)

Jacques Berthier

Principal Canon

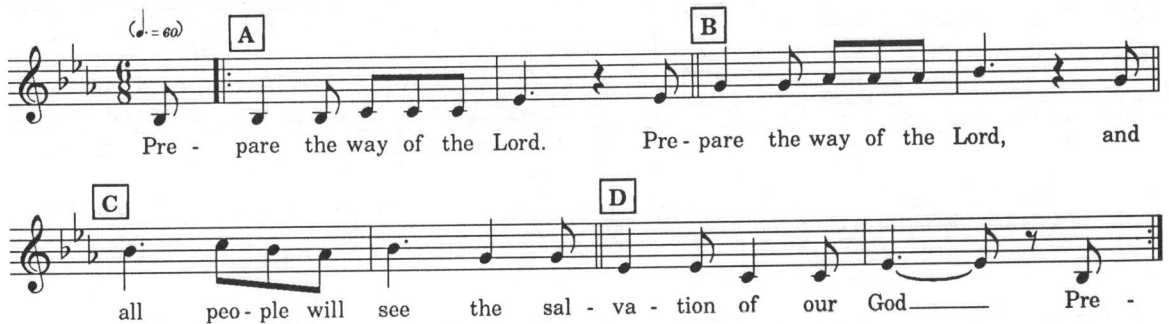

Pre - pare the way of the Lord. Pre - pare the way of the Lord, and

all peo - ple will see the sal - va - tion of our God_____ Pre -

Secondary Canons

1.
Al - le - lu - ia. Al - le - lu - ia. Al - le -

lu - ia. Al - le - lu - ia.

2.
Al - le - lu - ia. Al - le - lu - ia. Al - le - lu - ia.

Accompaniment

Keyboard or Guitar

E♭(D)   A♭(G)   E♭(D)

Chords in brackets: Capo 1

154 Into your presence

Peter Clark

Guitar chords an alternative to the keyboard accompaniment.

1 In - to your pres- ence, Fa - ther, we come with songs of re - joic- ing and praise. We are your Church, here gath- ered to - ge - ther, called for the rest of our days.

4 In - to your pre - sence, Fa - ther, we come with songs of re - joic - ing and praise.

(Ped.)
Em   Bm G A   Em Bm Am/C D Em Am⁷ B⁷

poco rit.

We are your Church, Lord, gath - ered to - ge - ther, called for the rest of our days.

E   B⁷ G♯m A   G♯m C♯m⁷ F♯m G♯ A maj⁷ B⁷ E

poco rit.

a tempo   *rall. . . . . .*

(Man.)   (Ped.)
E   C♯m B B⁷ A F♯m⁷ B⁷ E

2 We are your body working as one
     To bring your good news to the world.
     Here in your presence make us disciples,
     Make us your witnesses, Lord.

3 We are not worthy, we can do nothing,
     But that we do it in you.
     So, in your presence, Father, we ask you,
     Take us and make us your own.

155 Listen to the voice of the Lord (based on Psalm 94(95))

Patrick Geary

VOICE.

to Verses

Last time

Fine

rit.

G   G^sus   G   G^sus   G

Verse 1: *Cantor*   *mf*

Come, sing out— with joy   to the Lord;—   praise the

dim.   *mp*

G   G^sus   G   D/F♯   Em   Em/D

God who saves— us.—   With thanks-giv - ing come be-fore the Lord,

mf

Am   G/B   C   Am⁷   Am⁷/D   D⁷   G   Am

Refrain: *All*

f   *poco rit.*   *mf* D.S.

with songs let us praise— our God.—   O MY

D.S.

f   *poco rit.*   *mf*

C   Am⁷   F   Am   D^sus   D

5

6

hear the Lord,_____ do not hard-en your hearts_ as your

legato

F   Am   Bm⁷   Em

an- ces- tors did_ in the de - sert, when they doubt - ed,_though they saw God's work. O MY

Am   D   G/B   Em   C maj⁷   G maj⁷   Am⁷   D

Refrain: *All*
D.S. al Fine

Treble instruments I and II

Intro

mf

Refrain

f

Verse 1   7   *D.S.*

Verse 2   7   *D.S.*   **Verse 3**

6   *D.S. al Fine* | *Last time*   *Fine*

rit.

7

156 Gather us in
(Here in this place)

Marty Haugen

1 Here in this place new light is stream-ing, now is the dark-ness
va-nished a - way, see, in this space, our fears and our dream-ings,
brought here to you in the light of this day.
Ga - ther us in the lost and for - sak - en, gath - er us in the

blind and the lame; call to us now, and we shall a-wak-en,

D/F♯ G A D A C G

we shall a-rise at the sound of our name.

Gm/B♭ Dm C Am⁷ D C/D Gm⁶/D D

2 We are the young – our lives are a mystery,
   We are the old – who yearn for your face,
   We have been sung throughout all of history
   Called to be light to the whole human race.
   Gather us in the rich and the haughty,
   Gather us in the proud and the strong;
   Give us a heart so meek and so lowly,
   Give us the courage to enter the song.

3 Here we will take the wine and the water,
   Here we will take the bread of new birth,
   Here you shall call your sons and your daughters,
   Call us anew to be salt for the earth.
   Give us to drink the wine of compassion,
   Give us to eat the bread that is you;
   Nourish us well, and teach us to fashion
   Lives that are holy and hearts that are true.

4 Not in the dark of buildings confining,
   Not in some heaven, light years away, but
   Here in this place the new light is shining,
   Now is the Kingdom, now is the day.
   Gather us in and hold us for ever,
   Gather us in and make us your own;
   Gather us in all peoples together,
   Fire of love in our flesh and our bone.

157 Jesus calls us

Text: The Iona Community
*Tune: **Jesus Calls Us***
(Gaelic air adapted)

PENTECOST/CONFIRMATION

Responsorial Psalm Response

Send forth your Spi-rit, O Lord,— and re - new the face of the earth.

Gospel Acclamation

Alleluia Chorus

AL - LE - LU - IA, PRAISE THE LORD, AL - LE - LU - IA, PRAISE HIM.

CHRIST IS WITH US IN HIS WORD, AL - LE - LU - IA, PRAISE HIM.

2 Jesus calls us to confess him
Word of Life and Lord of All,
Sharer of our flesh and frailness
Saving all who fail or fall.
Tell his holy human story;
Tell his tales that all may hear;
Tell the world that Christ in glory
Came to earth to meet us here.

3 Jesus calls us to each other:
Found in him are no divides.
Race and class and sex and language –
Such are barriers he derides.
Join the hand of friend and stranger;
Join the hands of age and youth;
Join the faithful and the doubter
In their common search for truth.

4 Jesus calls us to his table
Rooted firm in time and space,
Where the church in earth and heaven
Finds a common meeting place.
Share the bread and wine, his body;
Share the love of which we sing;
Share the feast for saints and sinners
Hosted by our Lord and King.

158 Entrance Song

Alan Johnson

(Psalms 94(95) and 103(104))

LORD!

1 Come ring out your joy to the Lord; a
2 A migh - ty God is the Lord;
3 Come in, let us bow and bend low, let us
4 How ma - ny your won - ders O Lord! In
5 The glo - ry of God lasts for ever! May the

(At end 𝄐)

hail ___ the Rock who ___ saves us, let us come be - fore him giv - ing ___
great King a - bove all ___ gods, ___ in his hands ___ are the depths of the
kneel to the God who ___ made us, for he ___ is our God and ___
wis - dom you made them all, the earth ___ is full of your
Lord ___ re - joice in his works! May our thoughts ___ be pleas - ing to

thanks, with songs let us hail the ___ Lord.
earth, the dry ___ land he has ___ shaped.
we the flock that is led by his hand.
riches. Bless ___ the Lord my ___ soul.
him, we find ___ our joy in the Lord!

D.C.

D.C.

159 Sing Gloria

from Missa Gloria, a Mass for Ordination

Music and text adaptation:
Feargal King

Joyfully (c. ♩ = 152)

Ped. _ _ _ _ _ _ _ _ ❀ Ped. _ _ _ _ _ _ _ ❀ (simile)
A   Em⁷   Bm⁷   A

Cantor / Choir

Sing Glo - ri - a! Sing Glo - ri - a! Come and sing— in praise to the Lord our God! Sing Glo - ri - a! Sing Glo - ri - a! Come and sing— in praise to the Lord our God!

13

14

15

Coda

Sing Glo - ri - a to God!

Sing Glo - ri - a to God!

Sing Glo - ri - a to God!

F   G   A

Glo - ri - a!

Glo - ri - a!

Glo - ri - a!

Fine

B^sus4/A   Am⁷   D⁹/A   A

16

Verse 1 *Choir*

The ser - vants of God are ga - thered.

C   G   A

We bow as one be - fore his throne,

C   G   A

be - fore one Lord who is migh - ty,—

F   Em

the peo - ple of the Lord!

D.S.
(to Refrain)

F   Dm⁷   E   E⁷

D.S.

Verses 2 and 3

2 There is one Lord for us to wor-ship. There is one
faith for us to share. There is one God, one
Fa-ther, one spi-rit that we serve. *(To Refrain)*

3 His word goes forth to all the na-tions and brings good
news to the poor. to bind all hearts that are
bro-ken, to com-fort those who mourn. *(To Refrain)*

18

Instrumental duo

160 People of God

Peter McGrail

21

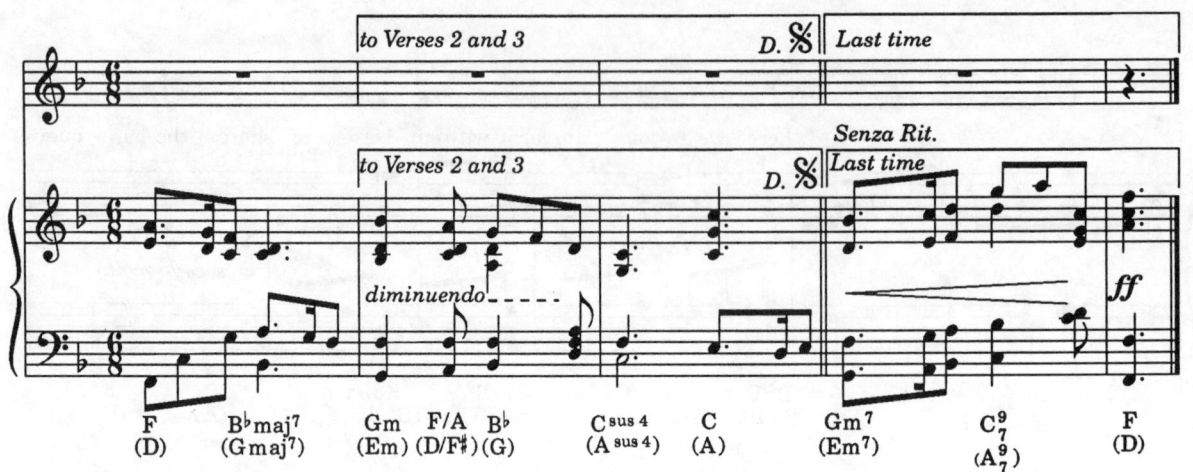

2 *(Cantor/Choir)*
Come with thanksgiving,
Hearts filled with gladness;
Come to rejoice in God's mighty deeds,
  God, the Maker of All!
Come with life's sorrows,
Bearing love's burdens;
You, who have known the mercy of God,
  Proclaim with us the Lord's forgiveness.

(Refrain/All)

3 *(Cantor/Choir)*
One in God's family,
Sisters and brothers,
Laying aside our fear and our pride,
  Here as servants to all.
One in our Saviour,
Sharing his story,
One as we eat the bread of new life
  And drink the cup of love and mercy.

(Refrain/All)

161 Entrance Psalm
from Mass of the Annunciation

Fintan P O'Carroll

23

Verse 4: Cantor and Choir (preferably men)

Praise the Lord, all you nations. Ac - claim him all you peo - ples.

Strong is his love for us: he is faith-ful for e - ver.

Al - le - lu - ia, al - le - lu - ia,

Organ ad lib. p

al - le - lu - ia,___ al - le - lu - ia!

A   Bm   F♯m   E   Bm⁷   F♯m⁷   D   E⁷ A

Choir and People unison

ff AL - LE - LU - IA,   AL - LE - LU - IA,

Gt.

ff

Ped. 8 + 16   A   F♯m   E   A   E   D   A   Bm   E

rall.

AL - LE - LU - IA,   AL - LE - LU - IA!

rall.

A   F♯m   E   A   E   D   A   Bm⁷   E   A

26

162 Lord, have mercy

Stephen Dean

from A Short Mass for Advent and Lent

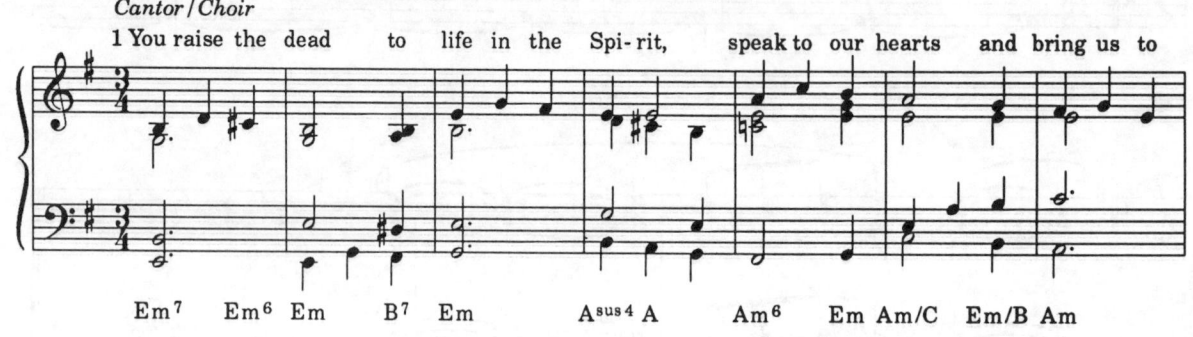

Cantor / Choir
1 You raise the dead to life in the Spi-rit, speak to our hearts and bring us to

Em⁷ Em⁶ Em B⁷ Em Aˢᵘˢ⁴ A Am⁶ Em Am/C Em/B Am

All
life. LORD, HAVE MER-CY, HAVE MER-CY, HAVE MER-CY, LORD, HAVE

B⁷/E Em Am D Em Am D B⁷ Em

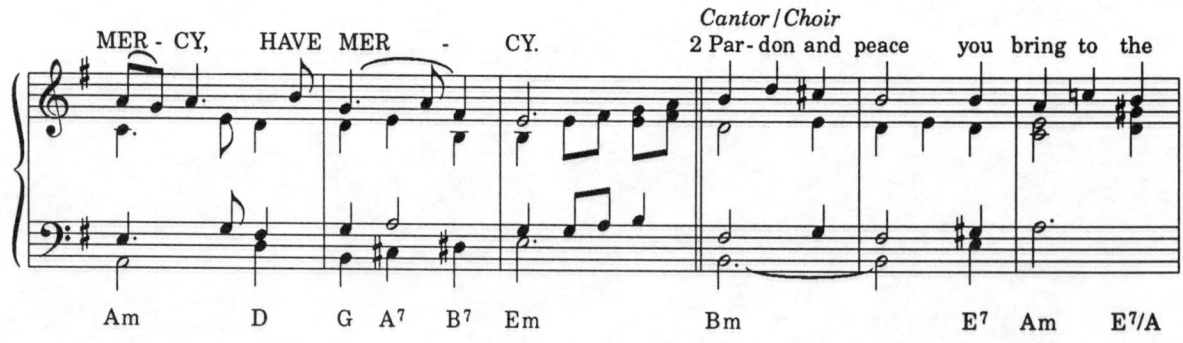

MER-CY, HAVE MER - CY. *Cantor / Choir* 2 Par-don and peace you bring to the

Am D G A⁷ B⁷ Em Bm E⁷ Am E⁷/A

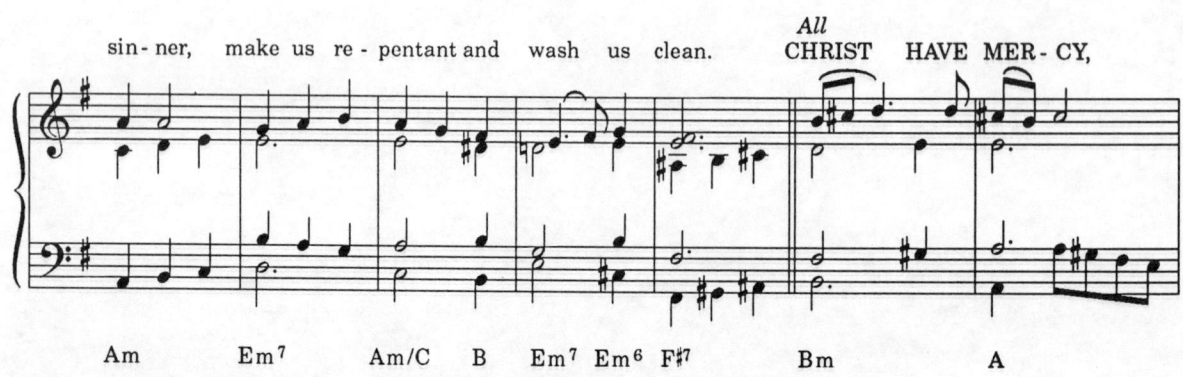

sin-ner, make us re-pentant and wash us clean. *All* CHRIST HAVE MER-CY,

Am Em⁷ Am/C B Em⁷ Em⁶ F♯⁷ Bm A

CHRIST, HAVE MER - CY, CHRIST, HAVE MER - CY, HAVE MER CY.

Dsus4   D7   G   Em   Em7/A   A7   D7   G   Amsus4   Am   Bm   Em

Cantor / Choir

3 You bring your light to those in the dark - ness, shine on us

Em   A7   D   D7   G   Em7   A   Bm   F#m   Bm

now, and wake us from sleep. LORD,___ HAVE MER - CY, HAVE

C#m   E7   F#m   Bsus4   B   Em   Am7   D

MER - CY, HAVE MER - CY, LORD,___ HAVE MER - CY, HAVE MER - CY.

G   C/E   Am6/E   B7/D#   Em7/D   Em6/C#   Am/C   Am6   Em/B   B7   Em

* Organists and guitar players may prefer to repeat the accompaniment for the first "Lord have mercy", bars 9–16.

29

163 Penitential Rite 2

for Choir (or Cantor)
and Congregation

Richard Jones

Choir: And grant us— your sal - va - tion.

All: AND GRANT US— YOUR SAL - VA - TION.—

If played on manuals only, omit upper G of L.H.
The sections for solo and choir may be redistributed as necessary.
If there is no choir, the cantor should sing those sections also.

164 Chant for Penitential Rite 3

Robert Sherlaw Johnson

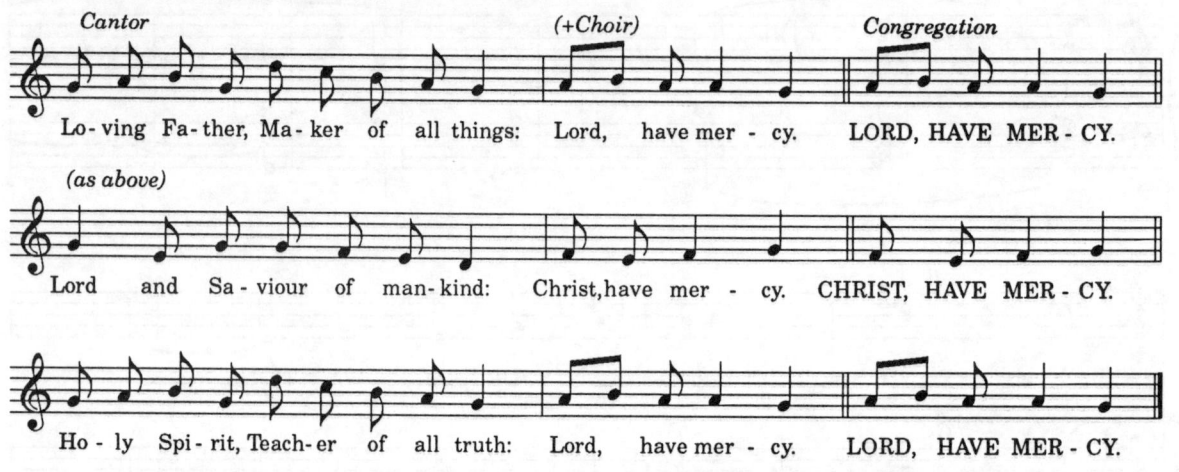

Cantor: Lo-ving Fa-ther, Ma-ker of all things: (+Choir) Lord, have mer - cy. Congregation: LORD, HAVE MER - CY.

(as above) Lord and Sa-viour of man-kind: Christ, have mer - cy. CHRIST, HAVE MER - CY.

Ho-ly Spi-rit, Teach-er of all truth: Lord, have mer - cy. LORD, HAVE MER - CY.

165 Penitential Rite: Jesus, born for us

Alan Smith

Cantor/Choir: Je - sus, born for us: Lord,—— have mer - cy.

All: JE - SUS, BORN FOR US:

Organ

166 White Light Kyrie

David Ogden

1,3 Lord have mer-cy.
2 Christ, have mer-cy.

LORD, HAVE MER-CY. LORD, HAVE MER-CY UP-ON US ALL.
CHRIST, HAVE MER-CY. CHRIST, HAVE MER-CY UP-ON US ALL.

ALL. (May almighty God have mercy on us, forgive us our sins, and bring us to everlasting life. AMEN.)

If this piece is being sung straight through without the priest's petitions then you may wish to repeat from the sign instead of from the beginning.

167 The Barnet Gloria

John Ainslie

Note: This Gloria is so arranged that it may be sung responsorially, Cantor/Choir (small letters) alternating with People (capitals), especially whilst it is being introduced to a parish. When it is well known it may be sung throughout by all.

168 Gloria

Mike Anderson

2 Jesus, Saviour of all, Lord God, Lamb of God,
  you take away our sins, Oh Lord, have mercy on us all.

3 At the Father's right hand, Lord receive our prayer,
  for you alone are the Holy One, and you alone are Lord.

4 Glory Father and Son, Glory Holy Spirit,
  to you we raise our hands up high, we glorify your name.

169 Glory to God

Ray d'Inverno

from A Children's Mass

Refrain *First time Cantor/Choir, All repeat. For Choir harmony, see page 39.*
Lively

Glo-ry to God, Glo-ry to God, Glo-ry to God in the high-est,

Last time

Glo-ry to God, Glo-ry to God, peace to his peo-ple on earth.

Verses *All (Choir harmony page 39)*

1. Lord God, heav-en-ly King, al-migh-ty God and Fa-ther, we

Refrain

wor-ship you, we give you thanks, we praise you for your glo-ry.

2. Lord Je-sus Christ, on-ly Son, Lord God, Lamb of God,

Refrain

you take a-way the sin of the world, have mer-cy, have mer-cy on us.

3. You're sea-ted at the right hand of God, Je-sus re-ceive our

Refrain

pray-er. For you a-lone are the Ho-ly One, you a-lone are the Lord.

4. For you a-lone are the Most High, Je-sus, Je-sus Christ,

Refrain

with the Ho-ly Spi-rit in the glo-ry of God the Fa-ther.

38

First time Cantor / Choir unison, All repeat (choir harmony)

high - est. A - men we say, A - men we say. Peace to his peo-ple on

earth. A - men we say, A - men we say. Glo-ry to God in the

Allargando

high - est. A - men we say, A - men we say. Peace to his peo-ple on earth.

Keyboards (Guitar) Refrain and verses

F	E♭maj⁷	F	A♭maj⁷	F/E♭	B♭/D	C⁷sus4	C⁷
Capo 3 (D)	(Cmaj⁷)	(D)	(Fmaj⁷)	(D/C)	(G/B)	(A⁷sus4)	(A⁷)

F	E♭maj⁷	Dm⁷	D♭maj⁷	B♭	C⁷sus4	F
(D)	(Cmaj⁷)	(Bm⁷)	(B♭maj⁷)	(G)	(A⁷sus4)	(D)

Coda

G	Fmaj⁷	G	B♭maj⁷	G/F	C/E	D⁷sus4	D⁷
(E)	(Dmaj⁷)	(E)	(Gmaj⁷)	(E/D)	(A/C♯)	(B⁷sus4)	(B⁷)

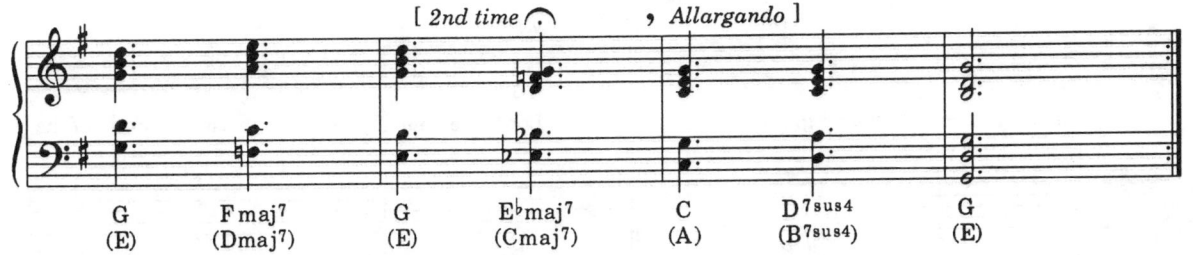

G   F maj⁷   G   E♭maj⁷   C   D⁷ˢᵘˢ⁴   G
(E)   (Dmaj⁷)   (E)   (Cmaj⁷)   (A)   (B⁷ˢᵘˢ⁴)   (E)

170 Gloria

Derek Fry

from Mass of St Edmund of Abingdon

Glo- ry to God in the high- est,—— and peace to his peo- ple on earth.—— Lord God, hea- ven-ly King, al- migh- ty God—— and Fa - ther, we wor - ship you, we give you thanks, we

praise__ you for__ your glo - ry. Lord Je-sus Christ on-ly Son of the Fa-ther,__ Lord God, Lamb of God, you take a - way the sin of the world: have mer - cy on us; You are__ seat-ed at the right hand of the Fa - ther: re - ceive our prayer. For you a - lone are the

Ho- ly One,— you a-lone are the Lord,— you a-lone are the Most High,

Je - sus__ Christ,__ with the Ho - ly Spi - rit, in the

glo - ry of God__ the Fa - ther. A - men, A - men.__

171 "Gifts" Gloria

Text: Patrick Lee
Music: Philip Gaisford

Light and rhythmical

All

GLO-RY TO GOD AND

E   A   Bsus 4 B   E   B

43

172 Gloria

Paul Inwood

from Shrewsbury Mass

Intro
With a swing ♩ = 69-72 (♪♪ = ♪ ♪ throughout)

Cantor / Choir

Glo - ry, glo - ry to God, glo - ry to God in the

Guitars: Capo 3
D⁷   G   C   G   C   G

high - est; glo - ry, glo - ry to God, glo - ry to God in the

Am⁷   D   G   C   G   C   G

high - est, and peace to his peo - ple on earth, and peace to his peo - ple on earth.

D⁷   G   C   G   Am⁷   D

* If only one instrument is available, the notes with stems down should be played.

Repeat **A** to **B**

49

you a - lone are the Most High, Je - sus Christ, with the Ho - ly

Em   A   D   D⁷   G   C

Spi - rit,   in the glo - ry of God the Fa - ther.

Am⁷   Dsus   D   G   C   Dsus4   D   *to* **C**

C

B♭ Trumpet

Optional instrumental descants

Optional choir parts

Glo - ry   to God,   glo - ry to God in the high - est;

All

GLO - RY, GLO - RY TO GOD,   GLO - RY TO GOD IN THE HIGH - EST;

G   C   G   C   G   Am⁷   D

173 Festive Gloria

Geoffrey Phillips

This Gloria is a congregational setting. Initially it will be sung responsorially. Later, when the people are familiar with it, they may join in throughout, omitting the sections in square brackets.

Part II · Liturgy of the Word

II · 1 Gospel Acclamations

174 Alleluias

Harold Barker

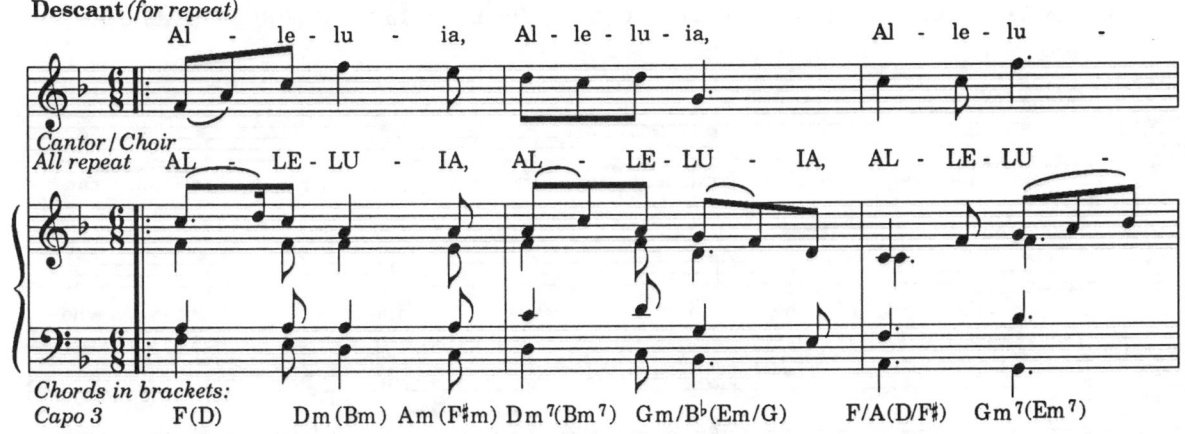

Descant *(for repeat)*

Al - le - lu - ia, Al - le - lu - ia, Al - le - lu -

Cantor / Choir
All repeat AL - LE - LU - IA, AL - LE - LU - IA, AL - LE - LU -

Chords in brackets:
Capo 3   F(D)   Dm(Bm) Am(F♯m) Dm⁷(Bm⁷) Gm/B♭(Em/G)   F/A(D/F♯)   Gm⁷(Em⁷)

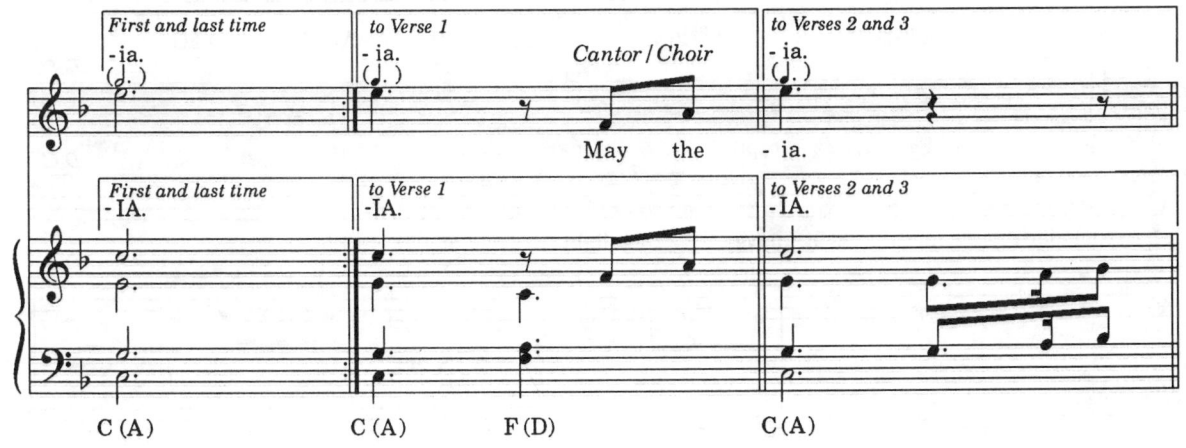

First and last time
-ia.
(♩.)

to Verse 1
- ia.
(♩.)
    Cantor / Choir

to Verses 2 and 3
- ia.
(♩.)

May the - ia.

First and last time
-IA.

to Verse 1
-IA.

to Verses 2 and 3
-IA.

C (A)   C (A)   F (D)   C (A)

Verse 1
Cantor / Choir

Fa - ther of our Lord Je - sus Christ——— en - ligh - ten the eyes of   our

F (D)   Gm⁷ (Em⁷)   C (A)   F/A (D/F♯)   B♭(G)

mind, that we can see what hope his call holds for us.

Am/C (F#m/A) F(D) Eb(C) Bb(G) C(A) Dm(Bm) Gm7/D(Em7/B) F/C (D/A) C(A)

Verse 2
Cantor / Choir

I am the Way, the Truth and the Life, says the Lord; no - one can

Verse 3
Cantor / Choir

I am the light of the world, says the Lord, those who

F(D) Gm7(Em7) F/A (D/F#) Bb(G) Am/C(F#m/A) F(D)

D.C.

come to the Fa - ther ex - cept through___ me.

D.C.

fol - low me will have the light of life.

D.C.

Eb(C) Bb(G) C(A) Dm(Bm) Gm7/D (Em7/B) F/C(D/A) C(A)

175 Alleluia

Tony Barr

The final Alleluia may be sung as a three-part round.

Tone

Al - le - lu - ia,___ al-le - lu - ia!

E Bm7 E Bm7 E Bm7 E Bm7 E Bm7 E Bm7 E Bm7

E Bm⁷ E Bm⁷ E Bm⁷ E Bm⁷ E Bm⁷ E Bm⁷ E Bm⁷

1 **2** **3**

Al - le - lu - ia,—— al - le - lu - ia!

E Bm⁷ E Bm⁷ E Bm⁷ E

176 Alleluia
for many Sundays

Geoffrey Boulton Smith

Allegro
Instrumental descant

All (First time Cantor/Choir, All repeat)
AL - LE - LU — IA, AL - LE - LU - IA, AL - LE - LU — IA,

G C⁶ G D/F♯ G
Capo 3 (E) (A⁶) (E) (B/D♯) (E)

AL - LE - LU - IA, AL - LE - LU — IA, AL - LE - LU - IA,

Am D E♭ B♭ C
(F♯m) (B) (C) (G) (A)

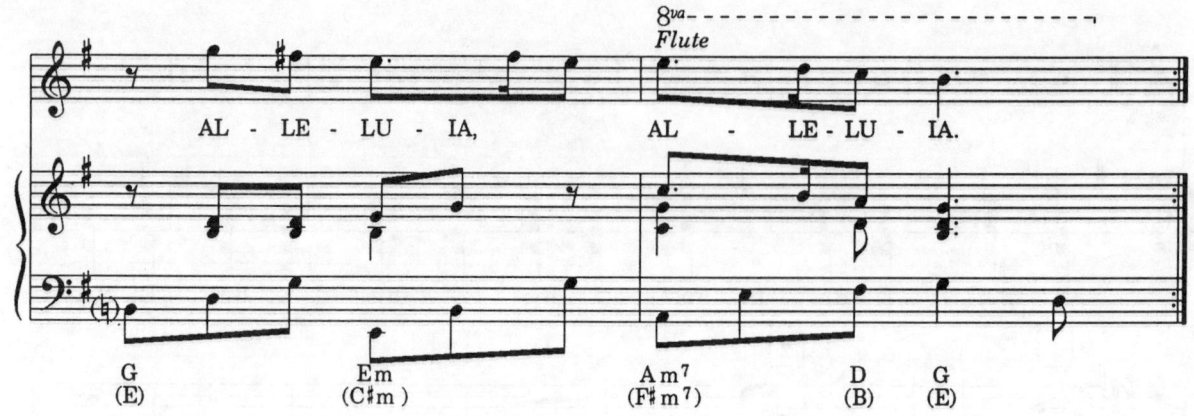

AL - LE - LU - IA,   AL - LE - LU - IA.

G   Em   Am⁷   D   G
(E)   (C♯m)   (F♯m⁷)   (B)   (E)

N.B. The arpeggio accompaniment in L.H. is more suited to piano than organ. Organists may prefer to prolong the quavers at the beginning of each beat to ♩. and omit the arpeggio figuration.

Verses *(choose one of 1-5)*
Cantor / Choir

*Omit

1 Speak,   Lord,   your ser - vant is

2 Your words are   Spi - rit,   Lord,   and they____ are

3 If   a - ny - one   loves   me   he will keep____ my

*Omit

4 O -   pen,   o - pen our

5 Your word is   truth,   Lord,   your word____ is

Vs 2,3,5 only

C   G   Am   G   C maj⁷   D m⁷
(A)   (E)   (F♯m) (E)   (A maj⁷)   (B m⁷)

* The first bar is omitted in acclamations 1 and 4.

177 Easter Acclamation

Stephen Dean

2 Come, risen Lord, walk beside us. . .
   May your Gospel ever guide us. . .

3 Open our hearts, risen Jesus. . .
   May your Spirit never leave us. . .

62

178 Praise to you, O Christ, our Saviour

Bernadette Farrell

B♭ trumpet

Refrain

Organ

Praise— to you, O Christ, our— Sav - iour, Word of the Fa - ther,

Em Bm Em   Am D Em   C G Am D

call-ing us to life;_____ Son__ of God who leads us to free - dom:

Em C Bmsus 4 Bm   Em Am Em Em7 Am D   G Em

1-4   *to Verses*   *Final*   *Fine*

glo - ry to you, Lord Je - sus Christ!   Christ!

C C/B Am Bm   Esus 4   Em   Em

Play cue size notes only when there is no trumpet available.

2 You are the one whom prophets hoped and longed for;
You are the one who speaks to us today;
You are the one who leads us to our future:
Glory to you, Lord Jesus Christ!

3 You are the Word who calls us to be servants;
You are the Word whose only law is love;
You are the Word-made-flesh who lives among us:
Glory to you, Lord Jesus Christ!

4 You are the Word who binds us and unites us;
You are the Word who calls us to be one;
You are the Word who teaches us forgiveness:
Glory to you, Lord Jesus Christ!

64

179 Alleluias

Gerry Fitzpatrick

Alleluia
Response

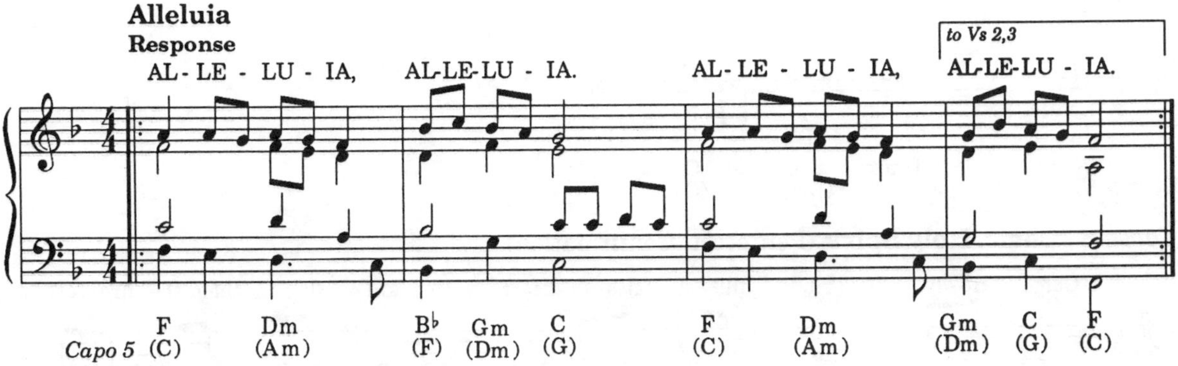

AL - LE - LU - IA,   AL-LE-LU - IA.   AL- LE - LU - IA,   AL-LE-LU - IA.

to Vs 2,3

Capo 5 (C)   F   Dm (Am)   B♭ (F)   Gm (Dm)   C (G)   F (C)   Dm (Am)   Gm (Dm)   C (G)   F (C)

to V 1   **Verse 1**

AL- LE - LU - IA.   Stay a - wake and stand read - y for you do not know the

Gm (Dm)   C (G)   F (C)   Dm (Am)   Gm (Dm)   C (G)

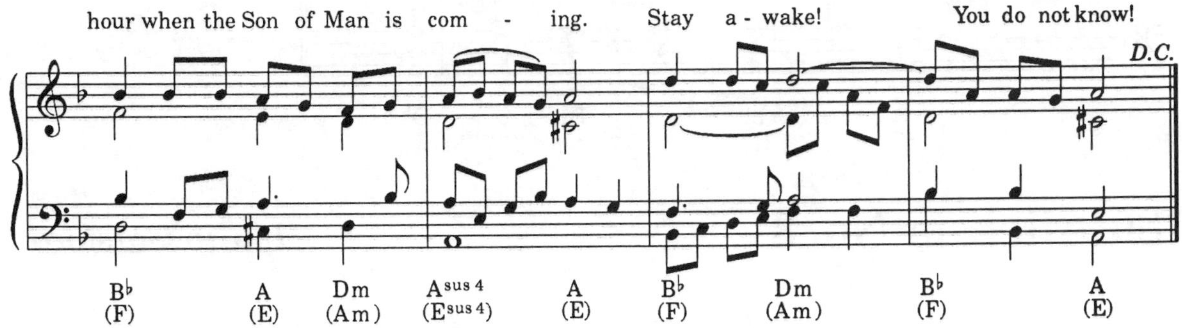

hour when the Son of Man is com - ing.   Stay a - wake!   You do not know!

D.C.

B♭ (F)   A (E)   Dm (Am)   A^sus 4 (E^sus 4)   A (E)   B♭ (F)   Dm (Am)   B♭ (F)   A (E)

(Uses: Verse 1: 32Y/A and B, 19Y/C, Suns end of year)

Verse 2 I am the way (Uses: 5 Eas/A, 18, 24, 29Y/B, 4, 11, 21Y/C, Suns of year)

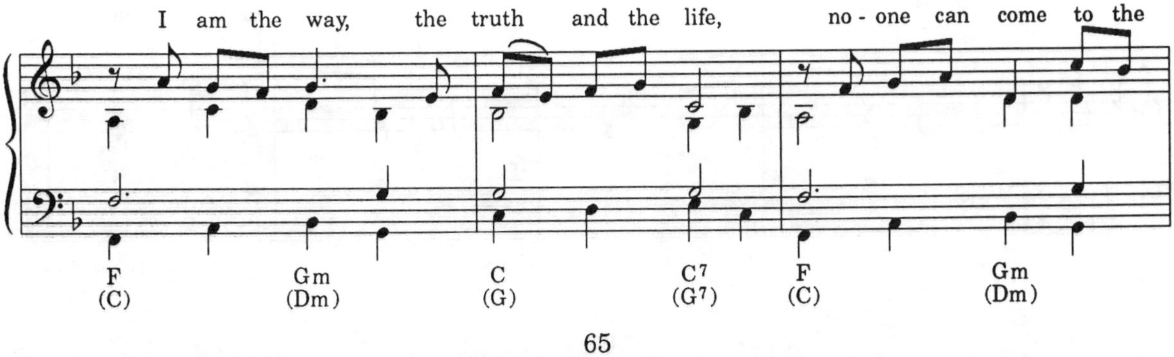

I am the way,   the truth   and the life,   no - one can come to the

F (C)   Gm (Dm)   C (G)   C^7 (G^7)   F (C)   Gm (Dm)

65

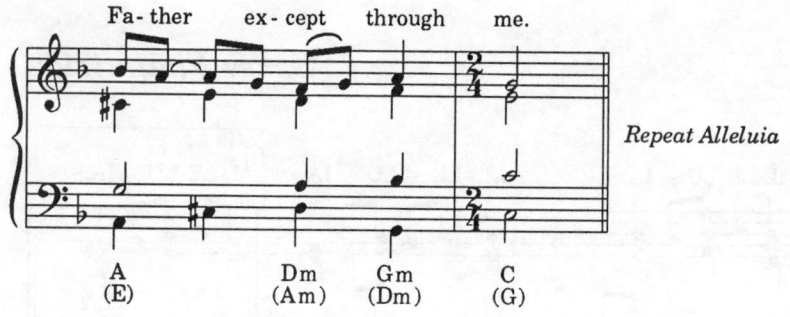

Fa- ther ex- cept through me.

Repeat Alleluia

A
(E)
Dm
(Am)
Gm
(Dm)
C
(G)

Verse 3 Come, Holy Spirit (Pentecost, Confirmation)

Come, Ho - ly Spi - rit, fill all faith-ful hearts, kin - dle in them the fire of

Dm
(Am)
Gm
(Dm)
C
(G)
B♭
(F)
A
(E)
Dm
(Am)

love. Come, Ho - ly Spi - rit, come.

Repeat Alleluia

A
(E)
B♭
(F)
Dm
(Am)
C
(G)
D
(A)

180 Alleluia No. 3

Philip Gaisford

B♭ *trumpet*

f

First time: Cantor / Choir, All repeat

più f

f Al - le - lu - ia, Al - le - lu - ia,

1,2
Last time
ff
Al - le - lu - ia. - ia.
D.C.
(mp)

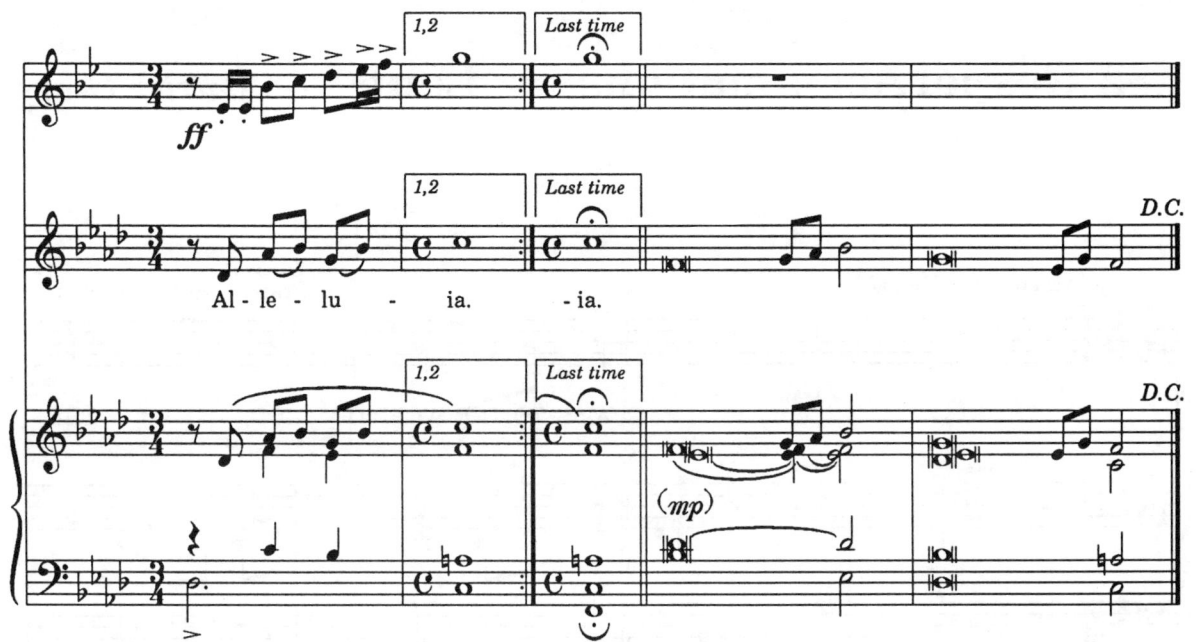

181 Alleluia No. 4

Philip Gaisford

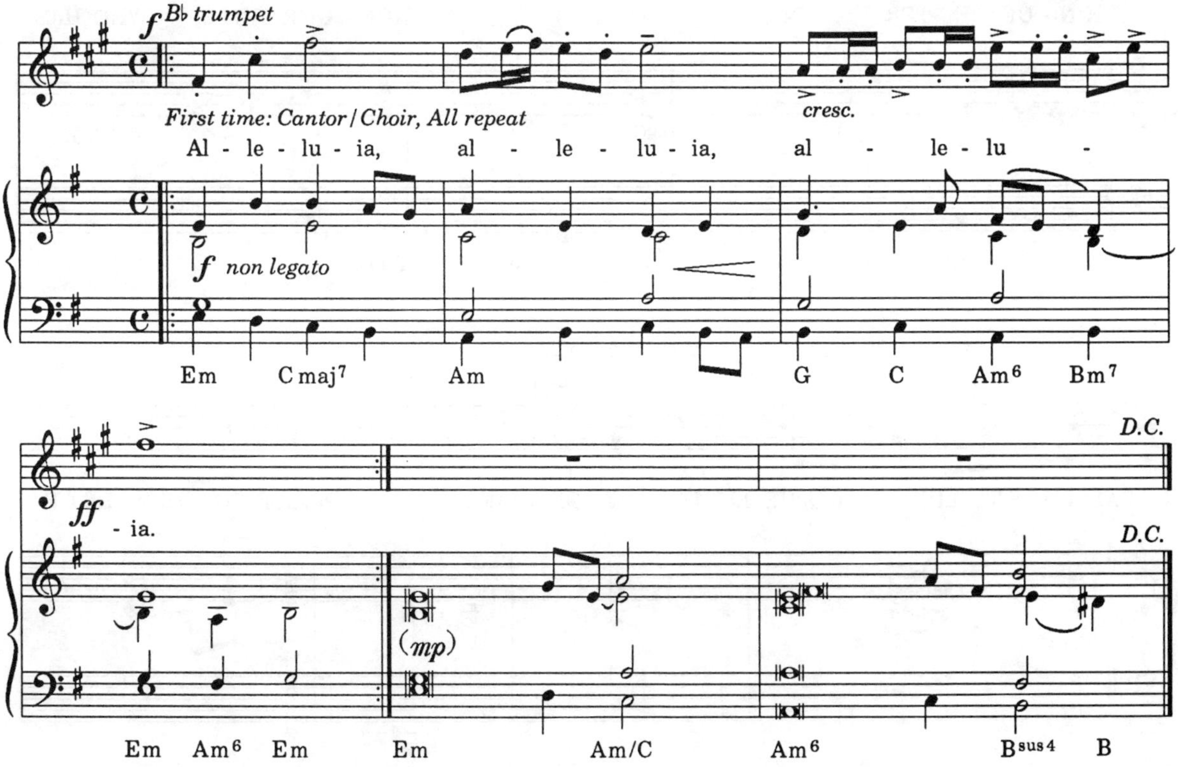

f B♭ trumpet
First time: Cantor / Choir, All repeat
cresc.
Al - le - lu - ia, al - le - lu - ia, al - le - lu - ia.
f non legato
Em C maj7 Am G C Am6 Bm7
ff
D.C.
(mp)
Em Am6 Em Em Am/C Am6 Bsus4 B

182 Gospel Acclamations for Lent

Patrick Geary

Praise to the Word of God, King of glo - ry. *to Verse*

GOD, THE KING OF E - TER - NAL GLO - RY. *to Verse*

Bm^sus   Bm   C   Am   Em

Last time
glo - ry.

1: Lent 2 (A/B/C); 2: Lent 3 (A); 3: Lent 5 (A), Lent 3 (B)

Cantor / Choir

GLO - RY.
Last time

1 From the bright cloud the Fa - ther's
2 Lord, you are the Sav - iour
3 I am the re - sur - rec - tion

E   Am   D   G

voice was heard: "This is my Son, the Be -
of the world. Give me your liv - ing
and the life. If you be - lieve in

C   A^sus   A   D/F#   Bm   *Dal %*

lov - ed. Listen to him."
wa - ter: so I will ne - ver thirst.
me you will ne - ver die.

Em   Em/D   C   Am   B   *Dal %*

69

Lent 1 (A,B,C)

Cantor / Choir

We can-not live by— bread a-lone,— but must live by the word of God.—

Am D G C Am D G² G

poco a poco cresc.

Praise to him— whose— pow-er in us— can do more than we know.

Dal 𝄋

poco a poco cresc.

C D G Em C Am B

183 Mantra Alleluia

Emmanuel Gribben

Ostinato Refrain

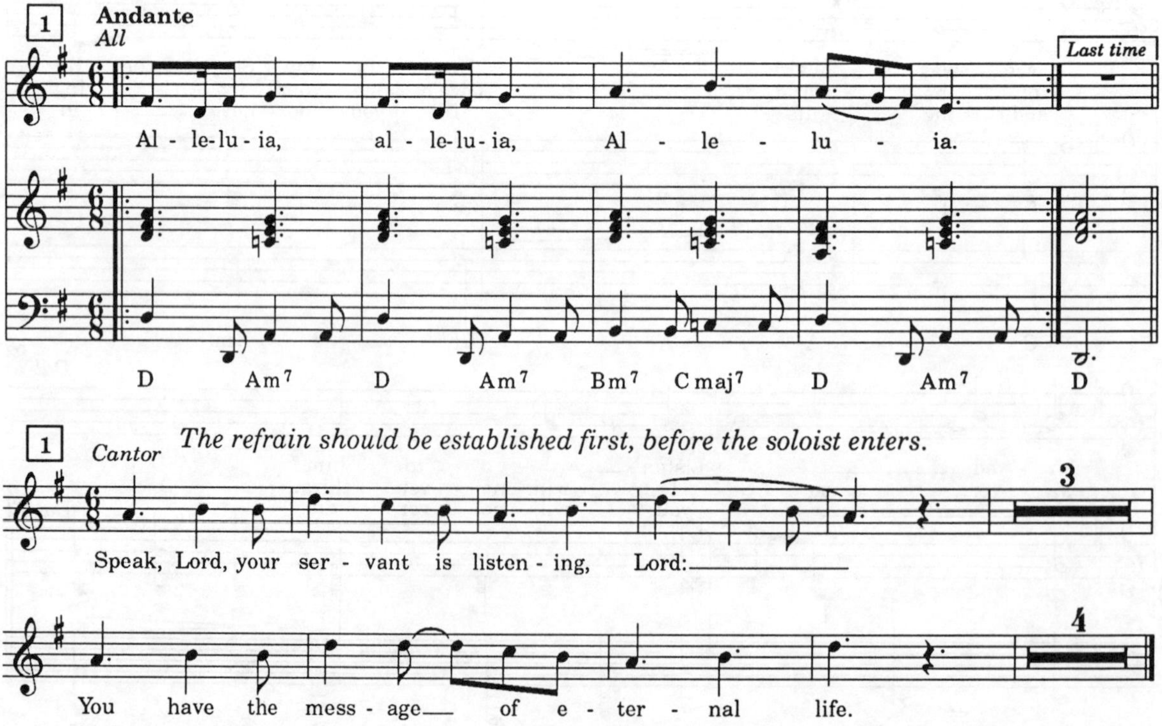

[1] **Andante**
All

Last time

Al - le-lu - ia, al - le-lu - ia, Al - le - lu - ia.

D Am⁷ D Am⁷ Bm⁷ Cmaj⁷ D Am⁷ D

[1] *Cantor* *The refrain should be established first, before the soloist enters.*

Speak, Lord, your ser - vant is listen - ing, Lord:—

3

You have the mess-age— of e - ter - nal life.

4

184 Alleluia: Easter Joy

From the plainsong
Arr. G Paul Johnstone

Refrain
Lively, joyful

AL - LE - LU - IA,—— AL - LE - LU - IA, AL - LE - LU - IA.——

Chords in brackets: Capo 3
Gm (Em) Dm⁷ (Bm⁷) Gm (Em) Dm (Bm) F (D) Gm (Em)

Easter: This day of days—— was made by the Lord, our hearts re-joice,—— our
General: Your word, O Lord, is a lamp for my steps, your word, O Lord, is a
O praise the Lord,—— Je - ru - sa - lem. He sends his word— to

Gm (Em) F (D) Gm (Em) B♭ (G) Gm (Em)

souls— are glad; we praise the Lord— who gives— us life. Al-le-lu-ia.——*R*
light for my path,—— by your word— you guide— my life. Al-le-lu-ia.——*R*
all— the earth. He is our God— and we— are his. Al-le-lu-ia.——*R*

Cm (Am) Gm (Em) C (A) Gm (Em) E♭ (C) Gm (Em) F (D) Gm (Em)

Descant

AL - LE - LU - IA, AL - LE - LU - IA, AL - LE - LU - IA.——

71

185 Alleluia

Peter Ollis

Holy Family and general use

AL - LE - LU - IA, AL - LE - LU - IA, — AL - LE - LU - IA.

Choir

May the peace of Christ — reign in your hearts; — let the

mes - sage of Christ find a home in you.   *Repeat Alleluia*

Repeat Alleluia

186 Alleluia

Alan Rees

from The Papal Mass at Cardiff, 1982

AL - LE-LU - IA, AL-LE-LU-IA. AL-LE-LU-IA, AL-LE-LU-IA.

AL - LE - LU - IA, AL - LE-LU - IA. I am the li-ving bread that has come down from

heav'n, says the Lord. A - ny-one who eats this bread will live_____ for e - ver.

187 Alleluia (Psalm 116(117)) *Christopher Walker*

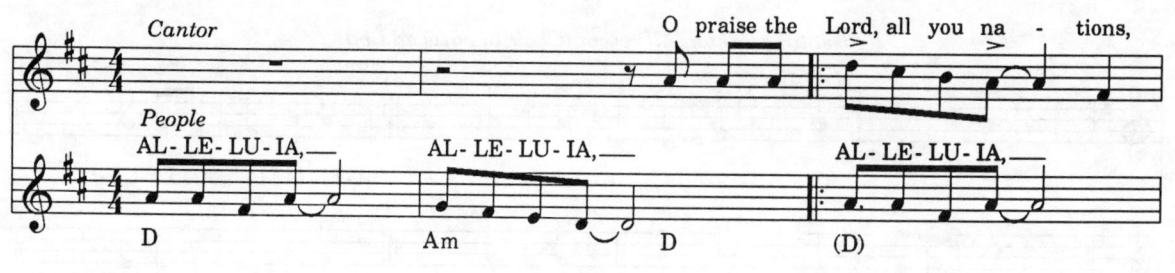

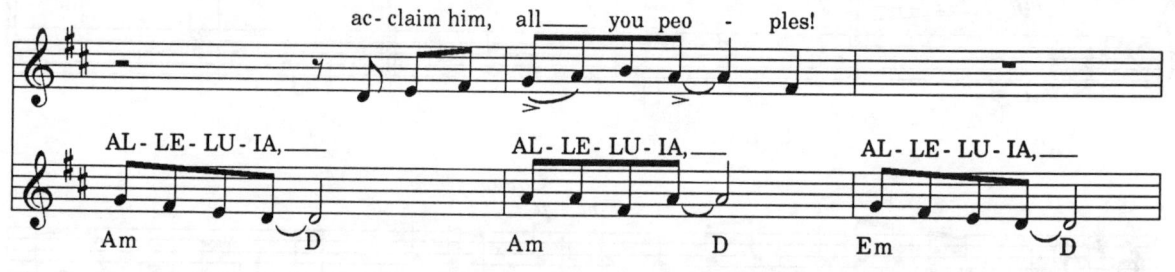

Note. This Alleluia is also the Responsorial Psalm for Sundays 9 and 21 of Year C.

188 Gospel Acclamation: Season of Lent

James Walsh

Praise—— to you, O Christ, king of e - ter - nal glo - ry!
or: Glo - ry to you, O Christ, you are the Word— of God!——

or: Glo- ry and praise to you,—— O Christ; glo- ry and praise to you,—— O Christ!

Tone

189 Advent Gospel Acclamations

Andrew Wright

* The people sing the soprano melody line.

al - le-lu - ia, al - le-lu - ia, al - le - lu-ia, al - le - lu - ia.

AL - LE-LU-IA, AL- LE-LU- IA, AL - LE-LU-IA, AL - LE - LU-IA.

F#m   Bm   Em   A   D   D⁷   Em   D

Verse texts

Advent 1

Let us see your mer - cy, O Lord,_____ your mer-cy, O Lord,_____

Advent 2

Pre - pare a way for the Lord,_____ make his paths_____ straight._

Advent 3

The Spi - rit of_____ the Lord_____ has been giv - en to me._____

Advent 4 (Yr A)

The vir - gin will_____ con-ceive_____ and give birth to a son_____

Advent 4 (Yrs B/C)

I am the hand-maid of_____ the Lord, the hand - maid of_____ the Lord:_____ let

mp

D   Bm   F#m   Bm   G   F#m   Bsus 4   Bm

77

and give us your sav - ing help, your saving help.

And all man-kind shall see the sal-va - tion,— the sal - va - tion of God.

He has sent me— to bring—good news, good news to the poor.—

and they will call him Em-man - u - el, Em - man - u - el.

what you have said be done— to me, be done— to me.

Adv. 2&3 only

Em   C   Am   D   G   D⁶   Em F♯m G   A^sus 4   A

78

190 We believe

1 Cor 15:3–5, 20–25

Graham Kendrick

With strength

1 We be-lieve in God the Fa-ther, ma - ker of the u - ni-verse,

Capo 2 F#m E F#m E F#m E^sus 4 E F#m E F#m E F#m E
(Em) (D)(Em) (D) (Em) (D^sus4) (D) (Em) (D)(Em) (D) (Em) (D)

and in Christ His Son our Sa-viour, come to us by vir - gin birth.

F#m E F#m E F#m E^sus 4 E F#m E F#m E F#m E
(Em) (D)(Em) (D) (Em) (D^sus4) (D) (Em) (D)(Em) (D) (Em) (D)

We be-lieve He died to save us, bore our sins, was cru - ci - fied.

A E A E A A^sus 4 A F#m E
(G) (D) (G) (D) (G) (G^sus4) (G) (Em) (D)

Then from death He rose vic - tor - ious, a - scen - ded to the Fa-ther's

A E A E A A^sus 4 A F#m
(G) (D) (G) (D) (G) (G^sus4) (G) (Em)

Chorus

side._____ Je - sus, Lord of all, Lord of all,_____ Je -

E (D)   F#m (Em)   Esus4 (Dsus4) E (D)   F#m (Em)   E (D)   F#m (Em)

sus, Lord of all, Lord of all,_____ Je - sus, Lord of all, Lord of all,_____

Esus4 (Dsus4) E (D) F#m (Em)   E (D)   A (G)   Asus4 (Gsus4) A (G) F#m (Em)   E (D)

Je - sus, Lord of all, Lord of all._____ Name a - bove all__ names.

A (G)   Asus4 (Gsus4) A (G) F#m (Em)   E (D)   F# (E)

Name a - bove all__ names._____

rit. Last chorus only

Name a - bove all__ names._____

E (D)   F#(E) (Em)   E (D)   F# (E)

2 We believe He sends His Spirit
On His church with gifts of power.
God, His word of truth affirming,
Sends us to the nations now.
He will come again in glory,
Judge the living and the dead.
Every knee shall bow before Him,
Then must every tongue confess.

191 Creed

Text arr. Crispian Hollis
Music: Christopher Walker

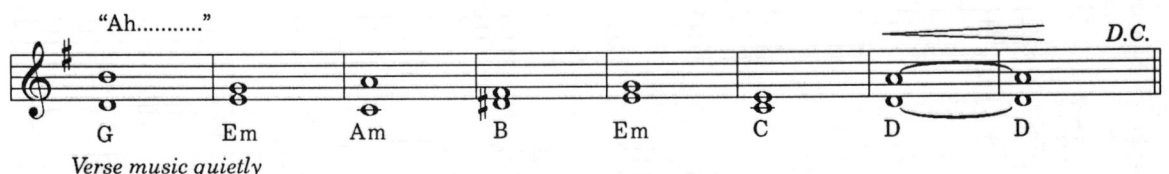

Verse music quietly

Verses *read by Celebrant/Reader:*

1 We believe in one God, the Father, the almighty,
maker of all that is, seen and unseen: WE BELIEVE. . .

2 We believe in the Lord Jesus Christ, God from God,
light from light; begotten not made,
one Being with the Father: WE BELIEVE . . .

3 Born of the Virgin Mary, he was crucified,
died and was buried. He rose again on the third day
and ascended to his Father in heaven: WE BELIEVE . . .

4 We believe in the Holy Spirit, the holy Catholic Church,
the communion of saints, the forgiveness of sins,
the resurrection of the body,
and life for ever with God in heaven: WE BELIEVE . . .

192 Music for the Intercessions

Liam Bauress

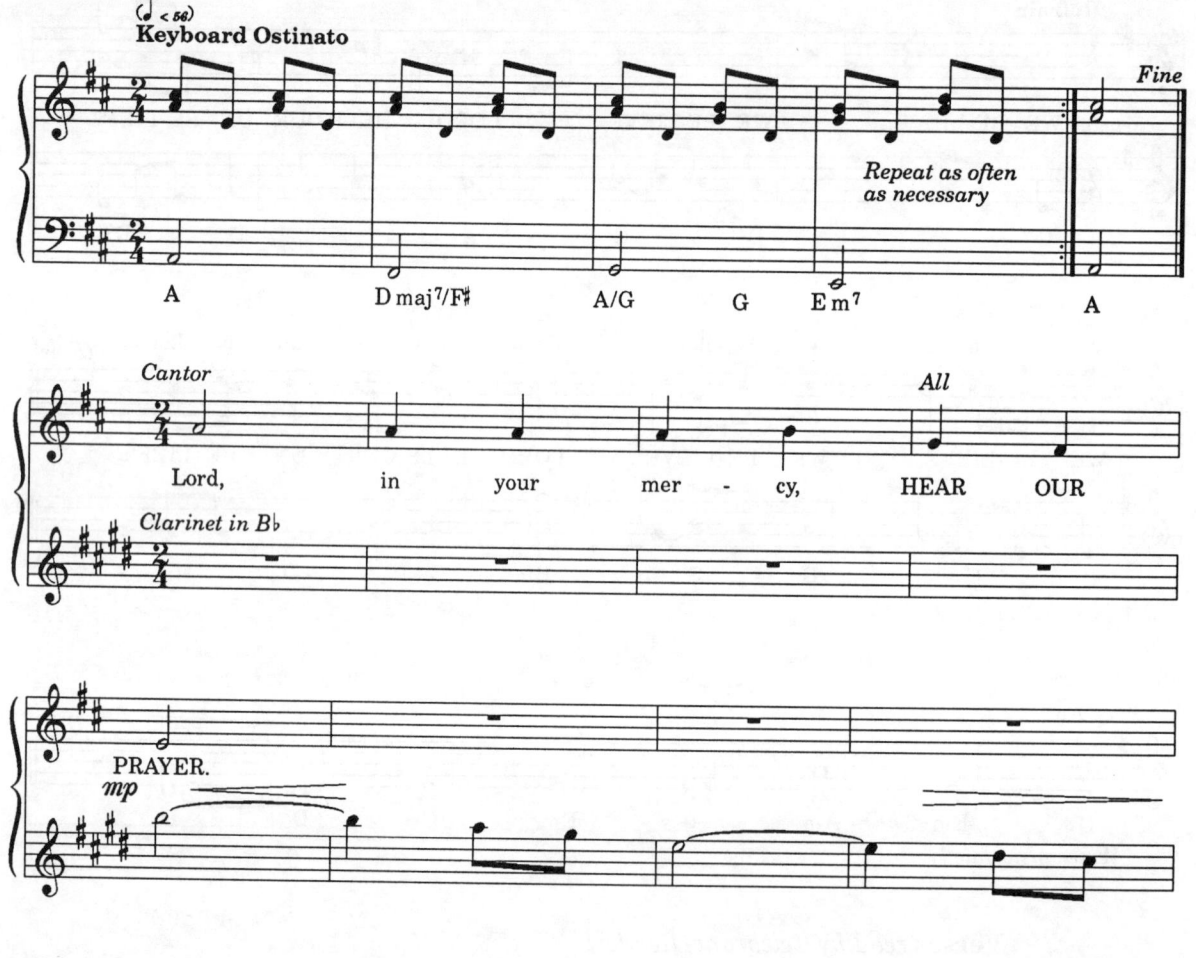

Notes on Performance

The organ (or other keyboard) part begins quietly before the start of the first spoken bidding prayer, which must not be rounded off by a spoken "Lord, in your mercy". The cantor enters in an unhurried way after the end of the spoken prayer, and the second bidding prayer should not start too soon after the clarinet stops playing. The four-bar ostinato figure in the organ part is played throughout, with appropriate crescendos and diminuendos, ending with a ritardando.

193 Intercessions

Gerry Fitzpatrick

Lord, turn to your peo-ple:_____ LORD, AN-SWER OUR PRAYER.

194 Prayers of the Faithful

from Missa Gloria

Feargal King

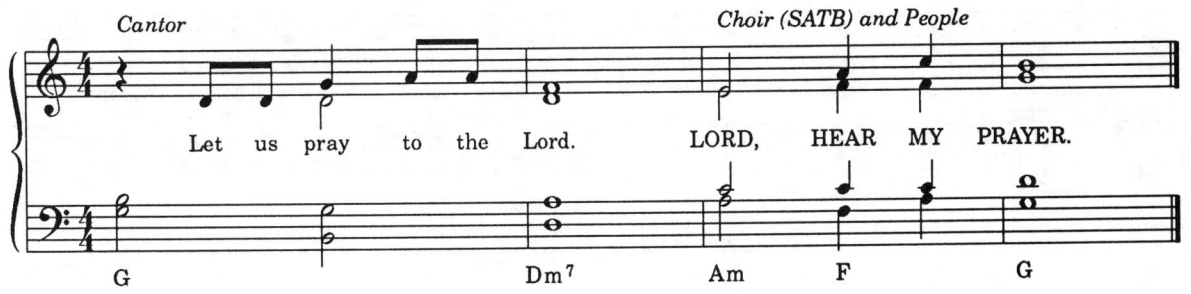

Let us pray to the Lord. LORD, HEAR MY PRAYER.

Part III · Liturgy of the Eucharist

III · 1 Preparation of the Gifts

195 All the gifts of God are holy

Text: Patrick Lee
Music: Bob Adams

* Play G sharp on third verse (E maj).

Soon his bo - dy men had bro - ken,— men whom Christ___ freed from the fall,— men whom Christ freed from___ the fall.

2 Next the cup of wine was taken, bless'd and giv'n as blood to share:
Blood soon shed by men unthinking, Christ, ignored, lay bleeding there.
Broken bread becomes the body, see, it is the risen Lord:
Wine new bless'd, he shares among us, Blood of Christ again outpoured,
Blood of Christ again outpoured.

3 Bread and wine once more we offer: Christ again will touch and heal,
Change our lives and make all holy; share with him this sacred meal.
All the gifts of God are holy, ours the hands which spoil and stain:
Offer'd to the Lord in tribute, Jesus' touch makes whole again.
Jesus' touch makes whole again.

196 A Christmas Offertory

Text: Patrick Lee
Music: Michael Coy
*(Tune: **Mair Wen**)*

In Beth-le-hem the house of bread— the wine of joy was— poured;_____ God made man came down— to earth; bless - ed be the Lord._____ bless - ed— be_____ the Lord.

2 Lord, this water mixed with wine
   is sign of human and divine:
   once more come down to earth and share
   divinity with us.
        In Bethlehem. . .

3 Lord we bring to you our wine,
   which through your goodness we possess:
   once more come down to earth and be
   the wine of life for us.
        In Bethlehem. . .

197 Preparation of the Gifts

Stephen Dean

from A Short Mass for Advent and Lent

fix our minds on you.

4 U - nite us in your love; and

by this ban - quet make of us one peo - ple in your sight.

198 Among us and before us

Text: The Iona Community
*Tune: **Gatehouse** (JLB)*

A - mong us and be - fore us, Lord, you stand with

G Bm Em Am⁷ Dsus⁴ D

arms out-stretch'd and bread and wine at hand. Con - front - ing those un -

G Em Am D⁷ G Bm

wor-thy of a crumb, you ask that to your ta - ble we should come.

Em Am⁷ Dsus⁴ D Bm⁷ Em Am⁷ D⁷ G

2 Who dare say No, when such is your resolve
   Our worst to witness, suffer and absolve,
   Our best to raise in lives by God forgiven,
   Our souls to fill on earth with food from heaven?

3 Who dare say No, when such is your intent
   To love the selves we famish and resent,
   To cradle our uncertainties and fear,
   To kindle hope as you in faith draw near?

4 Who dare say No, when such is your request
   That each around your table should be guest,
   That here the ancient word should live as new
   "Take, eat and drink – all this is meant for you"?

5 No more we hesitate and wonder why;
   No more we stand indifferent, scared or shy.
   Your invitation leads us to say Yes,
   To meet you where you nourish, heal and bless.

199 The Grail Prayer

Text: The Grail
Music: Andrew Wright

This song may be performed in a number of different ways. The melody may be sung by a soloist, or choir group, or even the whole Assembly, accompanied either by keyboard (organ/piano) or instrumental group. It may also be sung as a four-part SATB choir piece, unaccompanied.

peo - ple: all hu - man-kind,___ and I give you my whole self that
you may grow in me; so it is you, Lord Je - sus,
you, Lord Je - sus,___ you, who live and work and pray in

Em   A^sus 4   A   A^7   F♯m   D^7

G   Em   A   A^7   D

Em   A^7   D   G   Em

me, who live and work and pray in me.

(and pray in me.)

F♯sus 4 F♯ (no guitar) Bm Gm⁹ C/G D

200 Holy, holy

John Ainslie

* *Optional 'breather' bar*

† *Guitar chords are offered as an alternative if no organ is available. They should not be played with the organ part.*

201 Eucharistic Acclamations

Liam Bauress

1 Ho - ly, ho - ly, ho - ly Lord, God of pow'r and God of

Ho - san - na in the high-est, ho - san - na in the

Bless-ed is he who comes in the name of the

2 Dy - ing you de-stroyed our death, Ri - sing you re - stored our

3 A - MEN, A - MEN, A - MEN, A -

Flute/Recorder

Clarinet in B♭

Vocal Descant:

(Organ)

G   Am/G   C/E

might. Heav'n and earth

high - est, ho - san - na

Lord! Ho - san - na

life, Lord Je - sus,

MEN, FOR E - VER,

G/D   C   D/C   G/B

sing your glo - ry!_____
in the high - est!_____
in the high - est!_____
come in glo - ry!_____
A - MEN!_____

(rit. last time)

(rit. last time)

Vocal Descant:

(rit. last time)

Am⁷   C/D   D

202 St Andrew's
Responsorial Acclamations

Stephen Dean

202A Holy, holy

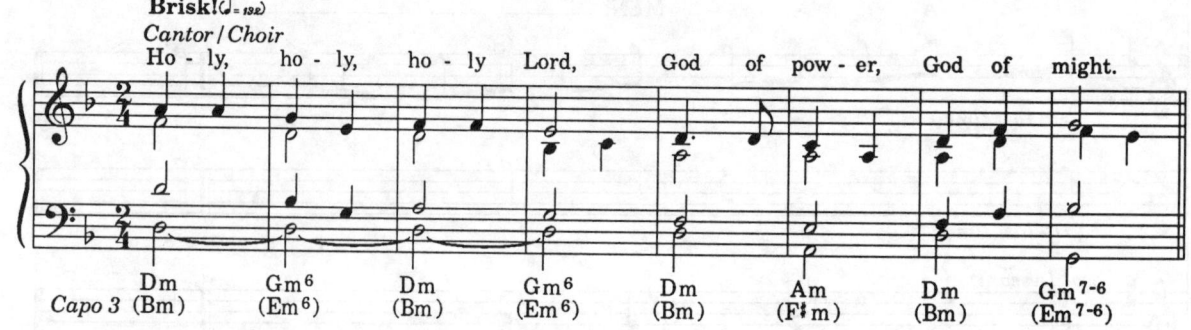

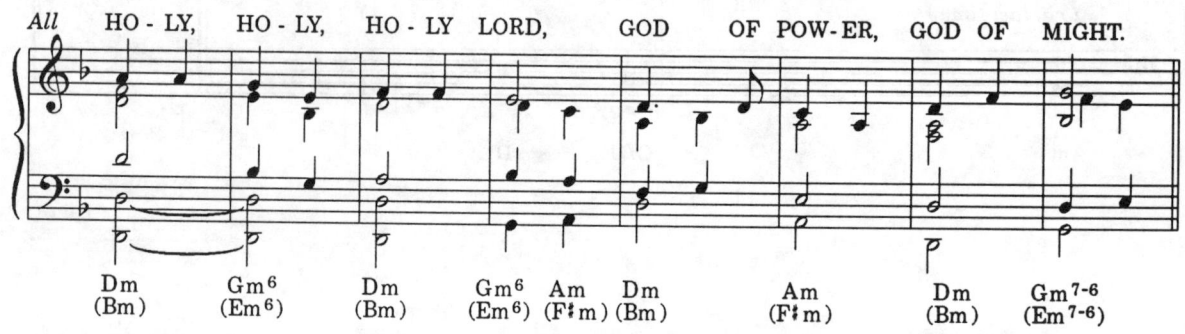

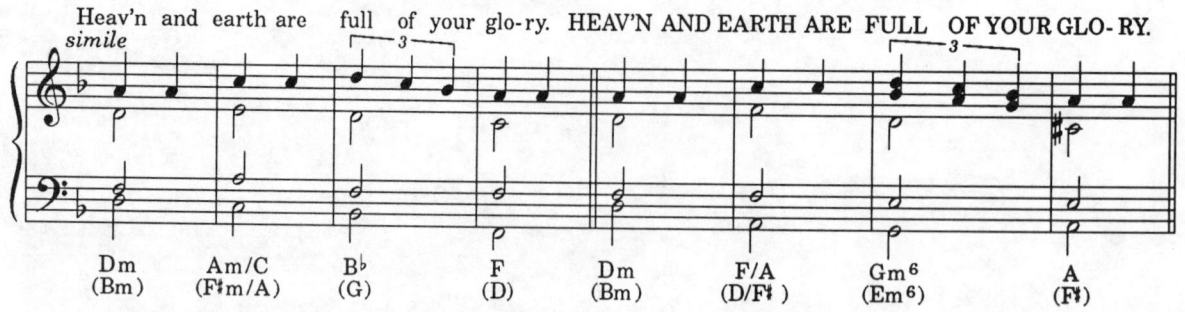

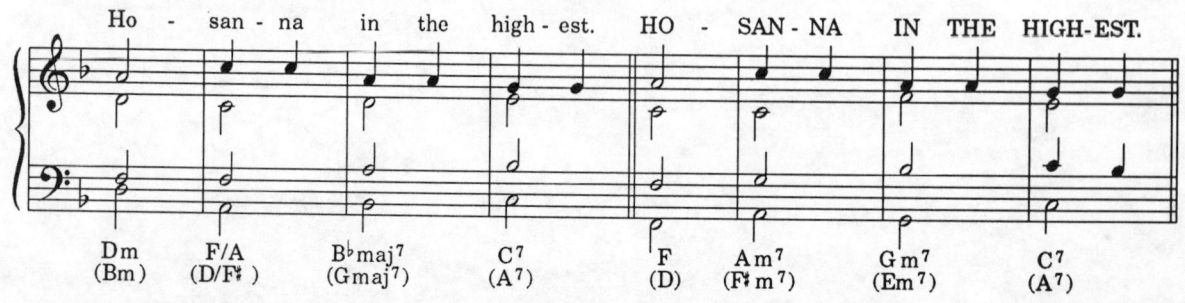

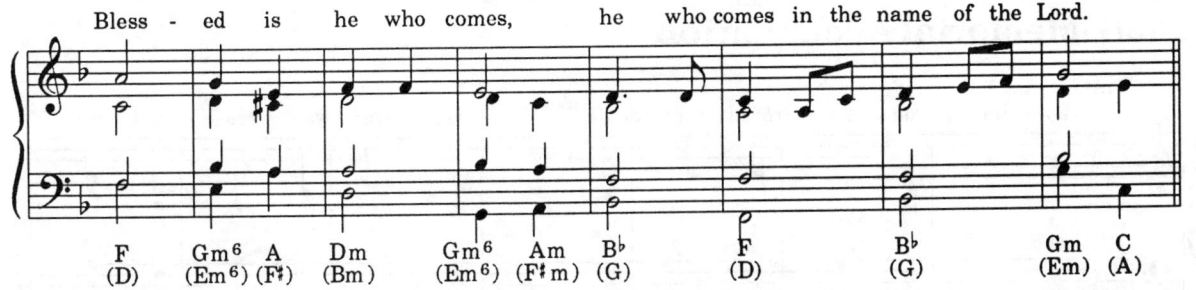

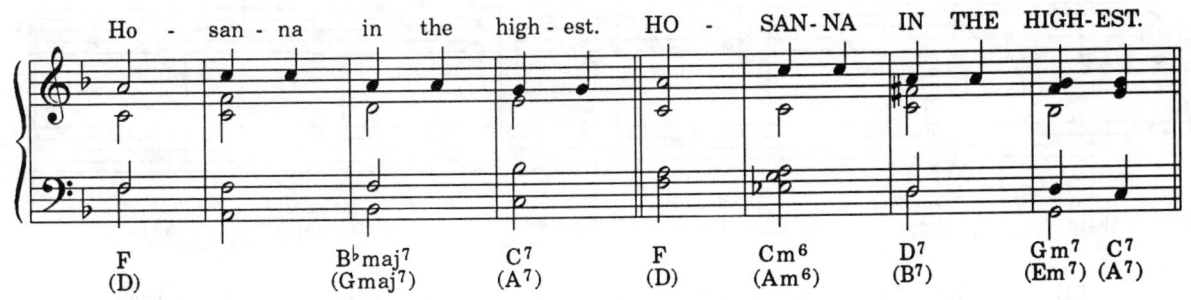

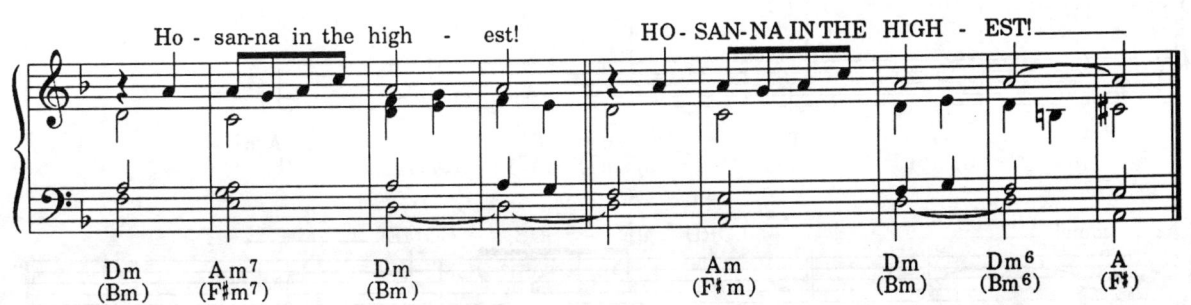

202B Memorial Acclamation

203 Eucharistic Acclamations

Bernadette Farrell

203A Holy, holy

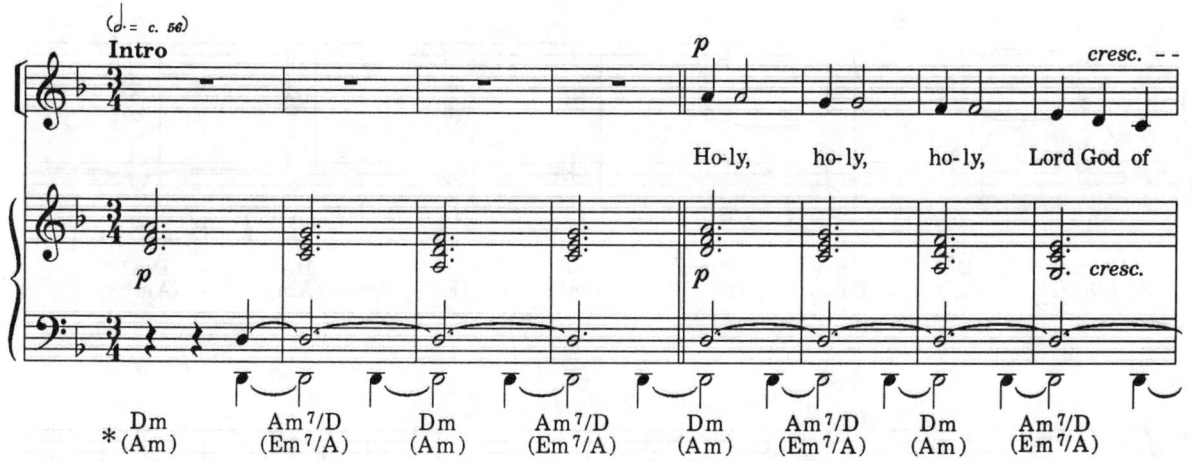

* Guitar chords as an alternative to organ accompaniment. Chords in brackets: Capo 5.

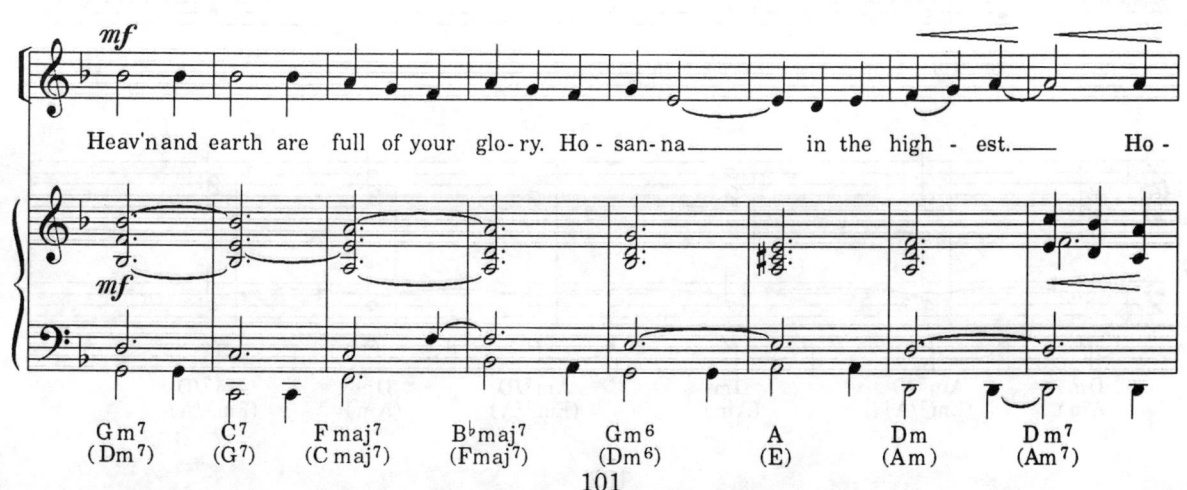

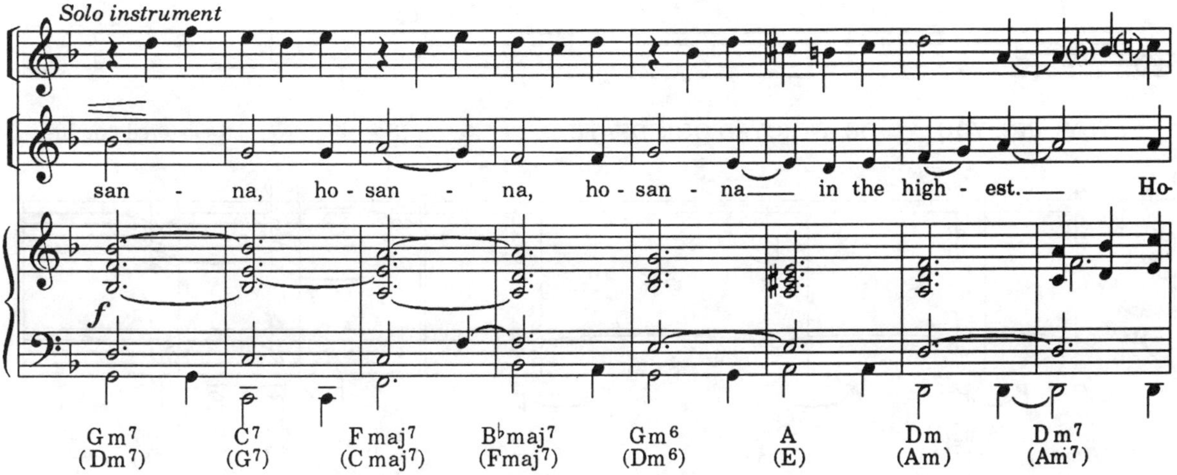
Solo instrument
san - na, ho-san - na, ho-san - na — in the high - est. — Ho-
f
Gm7 (Dm7) C7 (G7) F maj7 (C maj7) B♭maj7 (Fmaj7) Gm6 (Dm6) A (E) Dm (Am) Dm7 (Am7)

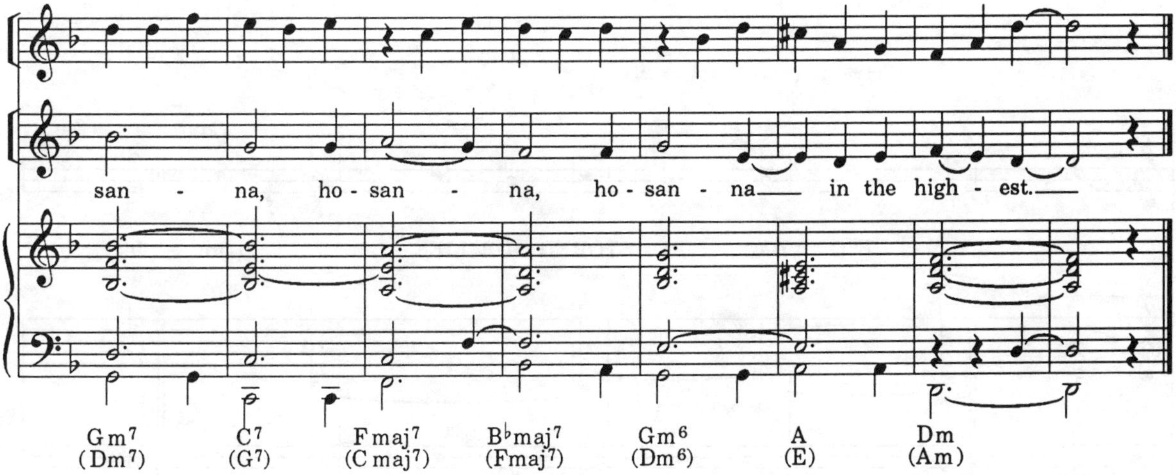
san - na, ho-san - na, ho-san - na — in the high - est. —
Gm7 (Dm7) C7 (G7) F maj7 (C maj7) B♭maj7 (Fmaj7) Gm6 (Dm6) A (E) Dm (Am)

203B Memorial Acclamation

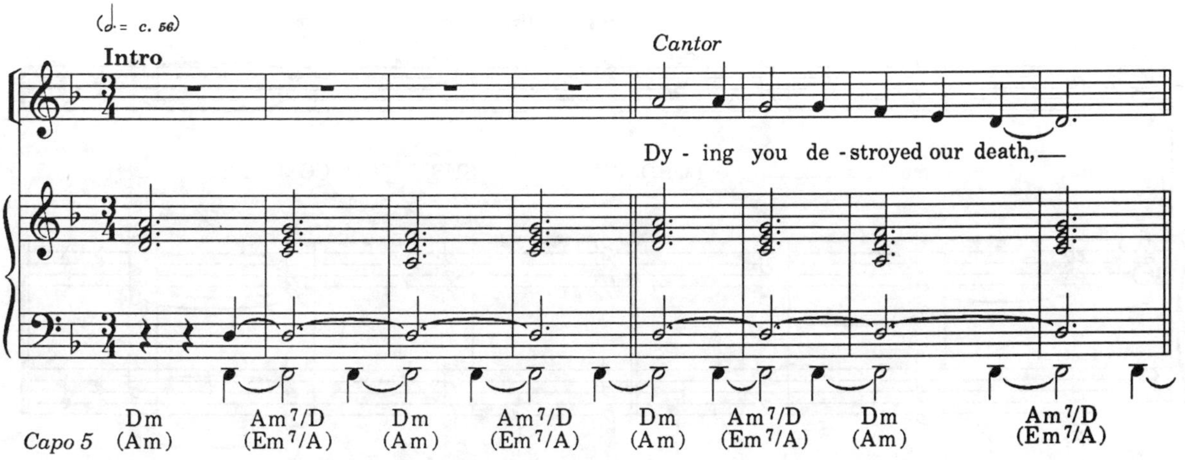
(𝅗𝅥. = c. 56)
Intro
Cantor
Dy - ing you de - stroyed our death, —
Capo 5
Dm (Am) Am7/D (Em7/A) Dm (Am) Am7/D (Em7/A) Dm (Am) Am7/D (Em7/A) Dm (Am) Am7/D (Em7/A)

DY - ING YOU DE -STROYED OUR DEATH,— Ri - sing you re - stored our life,

Dm   Am⁷/D   Dm   Dm⁷   Gm⁷   C⁷   Fmaj⁷
(Am)   (Em⁷/A)   (Am)   (Am⁷)   (Dm⁷)   (G⁷)   (Cmaj⁷)

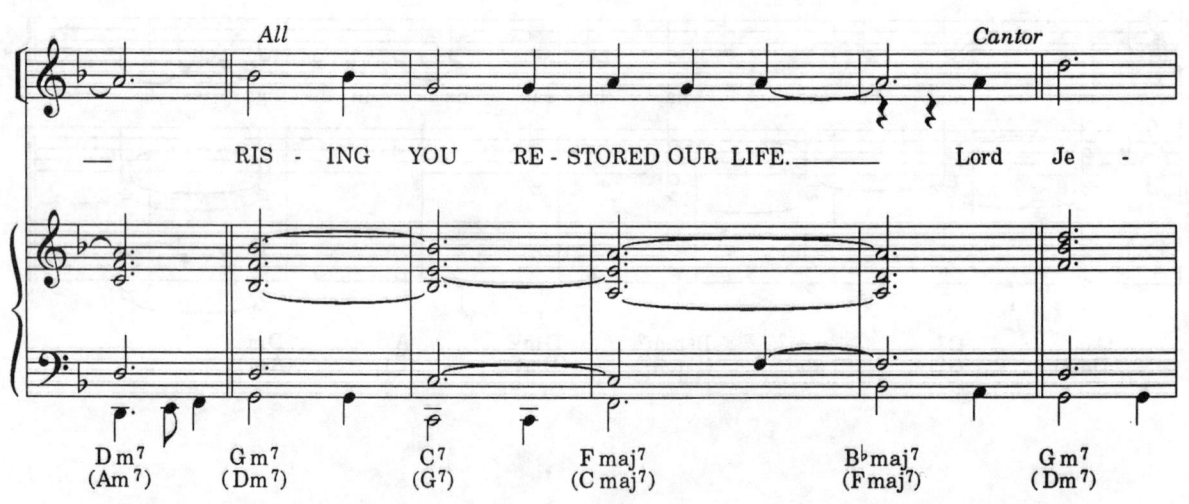

— RIS - ING YOU RE - STORED OUR LIFE.——— Lord Je -

Dm⁷   Gm⁷   C⁷   Fmaj⁷   B♭maj⁷   Gm⁷
(Am⁷)   (Dm⁷)   (G⁷)   (Cmaj⁷)   (Fmaj⁷)   (Dm⁷)

Cantor/Choir come in glo - ry.————
All

sus, come,——— LORD JE - SUS, COME.———

C   Fmaj⁷   B♭maj⁷   Gm⁷   Am⁷   D
(G)   (Cmaj⁷)   (Fmaj⁷)   (Dm⁷)   (Em⁷)   (A)

104

203C Amen *(when Doxology is sung)*

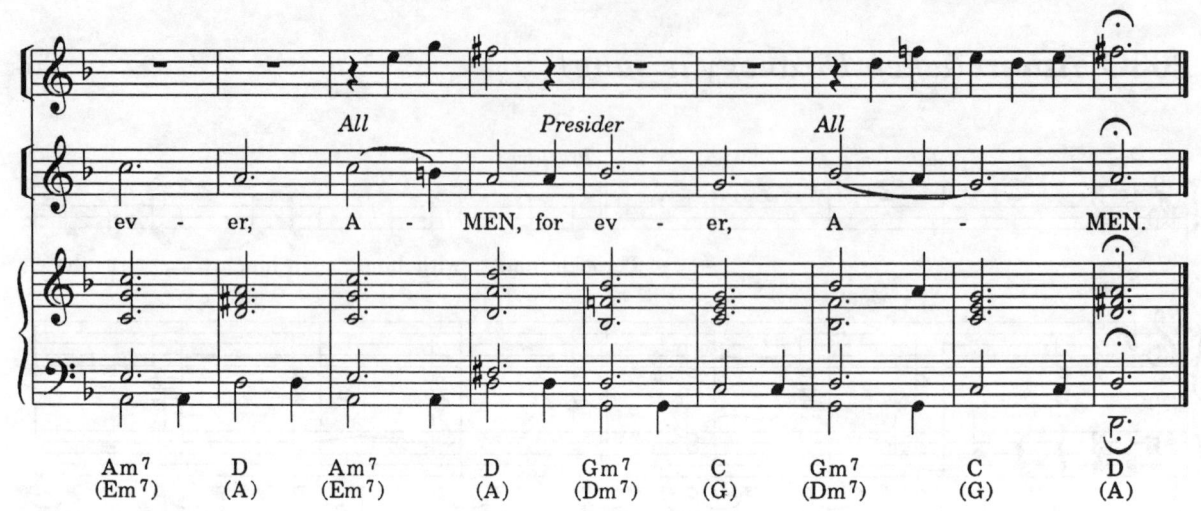

All · · · · · Presider · · · · · All
ev — er, A – MEN, for ev – er, A – MEN.

Am⁷ · D · Am⁷ · D · Gm⁷ · C · Gm⁷ · C · D
(Em⁷) (A) (Em⁷) (A) (Dm⁷) (G) (Dm⁷) (G) (A)

203D **Amen** *(when Doxology is spoken)*

Intro (♩· = c. 56)

Solo instrument

Cantor · · · · All · · · · Cantor
(...for ever and ever.) · A – men, · A – MEN, · A –

Capo 5 · D · D⁷ · Gm⁷ · C · Gm⁷ · C · Am⁷
(A) · (A⁷) · (Dm⁷) · (G) · (Dm⁷) · (G) · (Em⁷)

All · · · · Cantor · · · · All
men, · A – MEN, · A – men, · A – MEN.

D · Am⁷ · D · Gm⁷ · C · Gm⁷ · C · D
(A) · (Em⁷) · (A) · (Dm⁷) · (G) · (Dm⁷) · (G) · (A)

106

204 Eucharistic Acclamations for Children, Set A

Bernadette Farrell

204A We sing your glory

(Clap) We sing your glo-ry,— sing your praise, we sing your glo-ry,— sing your praise,

Capo 3 (D)
F (D) C (A) B♭ (G) C (A) F (D) C (A) B♭ (G) C (A)

we sing your glo-ry,— we sing your glo-ry.— Glo-ry, glo-ry and praise!

F (D) C (A) B♭ (G) C (A) F (D) C (A) B♭ (G) C (A)

This refrain can be used in two-bar phrases during the first part of the Eucharistic Prayer. A cantor should sing two bars, with everyone repeating them. The entire melody could then be sung and perhaps treated as a round at the time of the "Holy Holy", with entries at two bars' distance.

Amen

A - men, a - men.—

Capo 3 (D)
F (D) C (A) B♭ (G) C (A)

Alternative text for the "Holy, Holy":

We sing hosanna, sing your praise,
we sing hosanna, sing your praise,
we sing hosanna, we sing hosanna,
Glory, glory and praise!

This refrain of praise can be used again towards the very end of the prayer, and serves as the final response with the cantor singing the Amen, repeated by All (at will) and leading back into the round.

107

204B, C We are one body

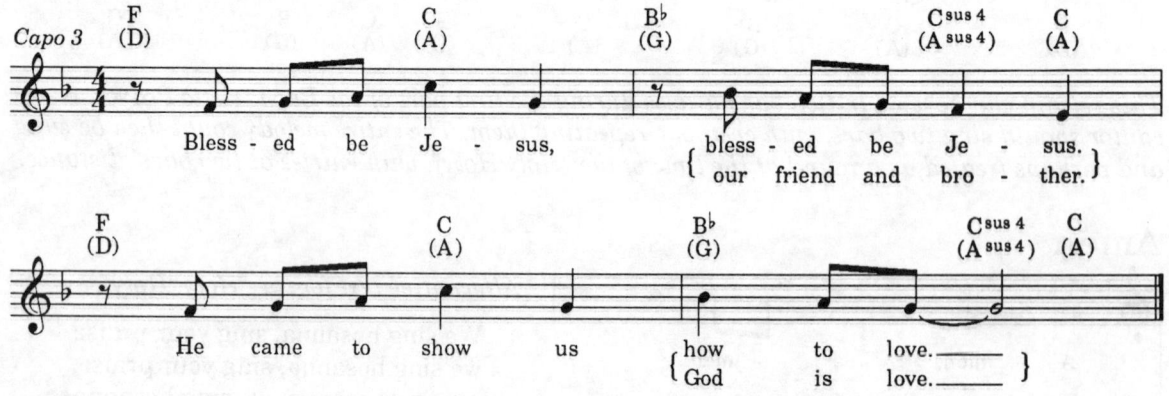

B Though we are ma - ny, we are one fam - 'ly,
C Make us your peo - ple, peo - ple of Je - sus,

Capo 3 (D)   (A)   (G)   (A sus 4)   (A)
      F   C   Bb   C sus 4   C

we are one bo - dy in your love.___
make us your peo - ple, called by love.___

(D)   (A)   (G)   (A sus 4)   (A)
  F   C   Bb   C sus 4   C

204D Blessed be Jesus

Capo 3 (D)   (A)   (G)   (A sus 4)   (A)
          F   C   Bb   C sus 4   C

Bless - ed be Je - sus, { bless - ed be Je - sus.
                        { our friend and bro - ther. }

(D)   (A)   (G)   (A sus 4)   (A)
  F   C   Bb   C sus 4   C

He came to show us { how to love.___
                    { God is love.___ }

This provides an additional response if one is needed. The first line may be used on its own, or with the additional/alternative words. Not every children's Eucharistic Prayer text includes an acclamation directly after the words of consecration, but this might be used as one if necessary. The accompaniment is as 204B, C.

204E Make us a sign of Jesus Christ

Cantor / Choir .... *All*

WORLD. Make us a sign of your great love— to the world. MAKE US A SIGN OF

Capo 3   F (D)   Dm (Bm)   B♭ (G)   C (A)   F (D)   Dm (Bm)

world. *Descant*   Make us a sign of Christ to the world.
Melody, *Cantor / Choir, All repeat*   *End*

YOUR GREAT LOVE TO THE WORLD. Make us a sign of Je-sus Christ in the world.   *End*

B♭ (G)   C (A)   F (D)   Dm (Bm)   B♭ (G)   C (A)   F (D)

Where appropriate, this third refrain can begin as written (Cantor / All overlapping) and build up through the following phrases, always culminating in the final phrase (even if the others are not used):

> Make us a sign of your great love to the world.
> Make us a sign of peace, a sign on the earth.
> Make us a sign of hope to those in despair.
> Make us a sign of light to those in the dark.
> Make us a sign of Jesus Christ in the world.

These refrains can be repeated after the cantor, or everyone can be divided into two halves, repeating the final phrase until everyone is singing it. The words (e.g. third, fourth lines) may be simplified.

A background ostinato can act as a focus for the spoken word, if played simply. The following examples are for CHIME BARS, and the children should count at least a slow "2" for each note.

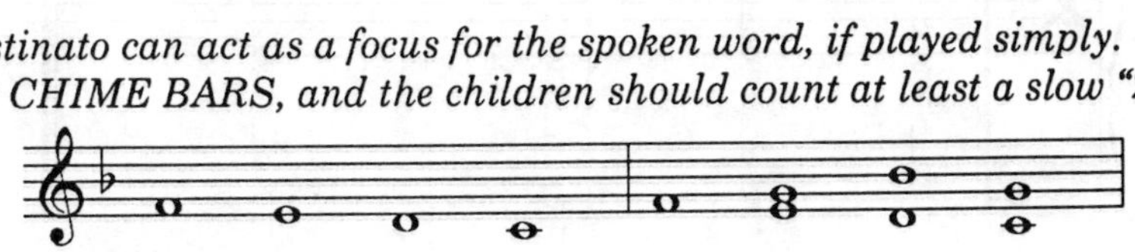

204F Doxology

205 Holy, holy
from Mass of St Edmund of Abingdon

Derek Fry

Ho - ly,— ho - ly,— ho - ly— Lord,

God— of— pow'r— and— might.————————— Hea - ven and—

earth are full— of your glo - ry. Ho - san - na, ho - san - na, ho -

san - na in the high - est. Bless - ed is he who comes— in the name of the

206 Eucharistic Acclamations with Children

Sue Furlong

206A Holy, holy

*Children

Ho - ly, ho - ly, ho - ly Lord, God of pow'r and God— of might.

G   G/B   Am⁷   D⁷   G   Am⁷   D

If there are adults and children present the children should sing this part on their own. The congregation and/or choir then join in the response, in unison or in two- or three-part harmony.

Other Acclamations

206B Acclamation 1

HO - LY, HO - LY, HO - LY LORD, HO - SAN - NA IN THE HIGH - EST.

206C Acclamation 2 and 206D Amen

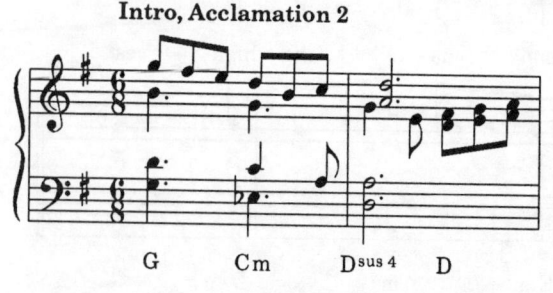

C Accl. 2 CHRIST THE LORD IS RI-SEN IN-DEED,} GLO-RY TO GOD IN THE HIGH - EST.
D   A   -   MEN,   A   -   MEN,}

G   D   Em   B⁷   Em   Am⁷   D⁷   G

Instrumental parts
206A Holy, holy

Flute

Other Acclamations (206B, C, D)

Note: A complete setting of Children's Eucharistic Prayer can be obtained from Sue Furlong (address in Acknowledgements).

207 Eucharistic Acclamations

Paul Inwood

from Gathering Mass

207A Holy, holy

Optional SATB Choir

119

207B Memorial Acclamation A

120

207C Memorial Acclamation B

rit.   *Fine*

san - na   in the high - est heav'ns!

rit.

rit.   *Fine*

NA,   HO - SAN -   NA IN THE HIGH - EST HEAV'NS!

Fine

rit.

Bsus4   Bm7   C   G/B   Am7   D   G

207D Doxology and Amen

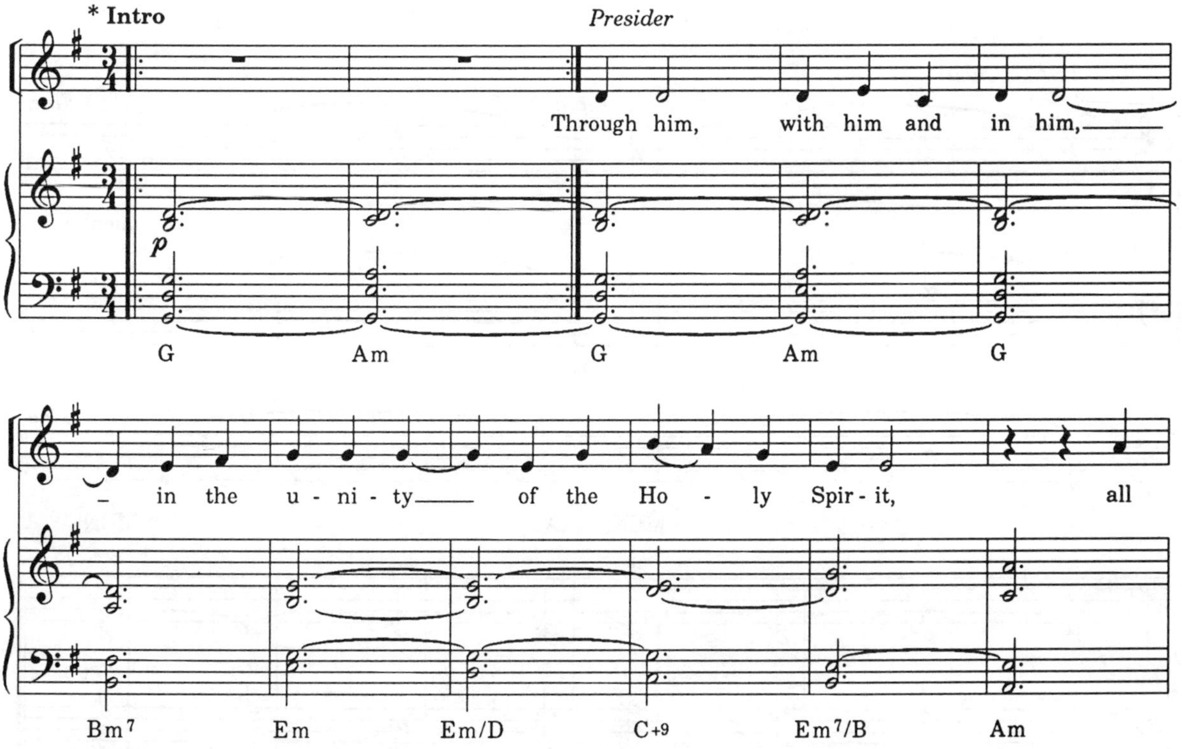

* Intro   *Presider*

Through him,   with him and   in him, ___

p

G   Am   G   Am   G

in the u - ni - ty ___ of the Ho - ly Spir - it,   all

Bm7   Em   Em/D   C+9   Em7/B   Am

* *If Doxology is spoken, repeat these two bars quietly underneath as many times as necessary, then go straight to the Amens on page 124.*

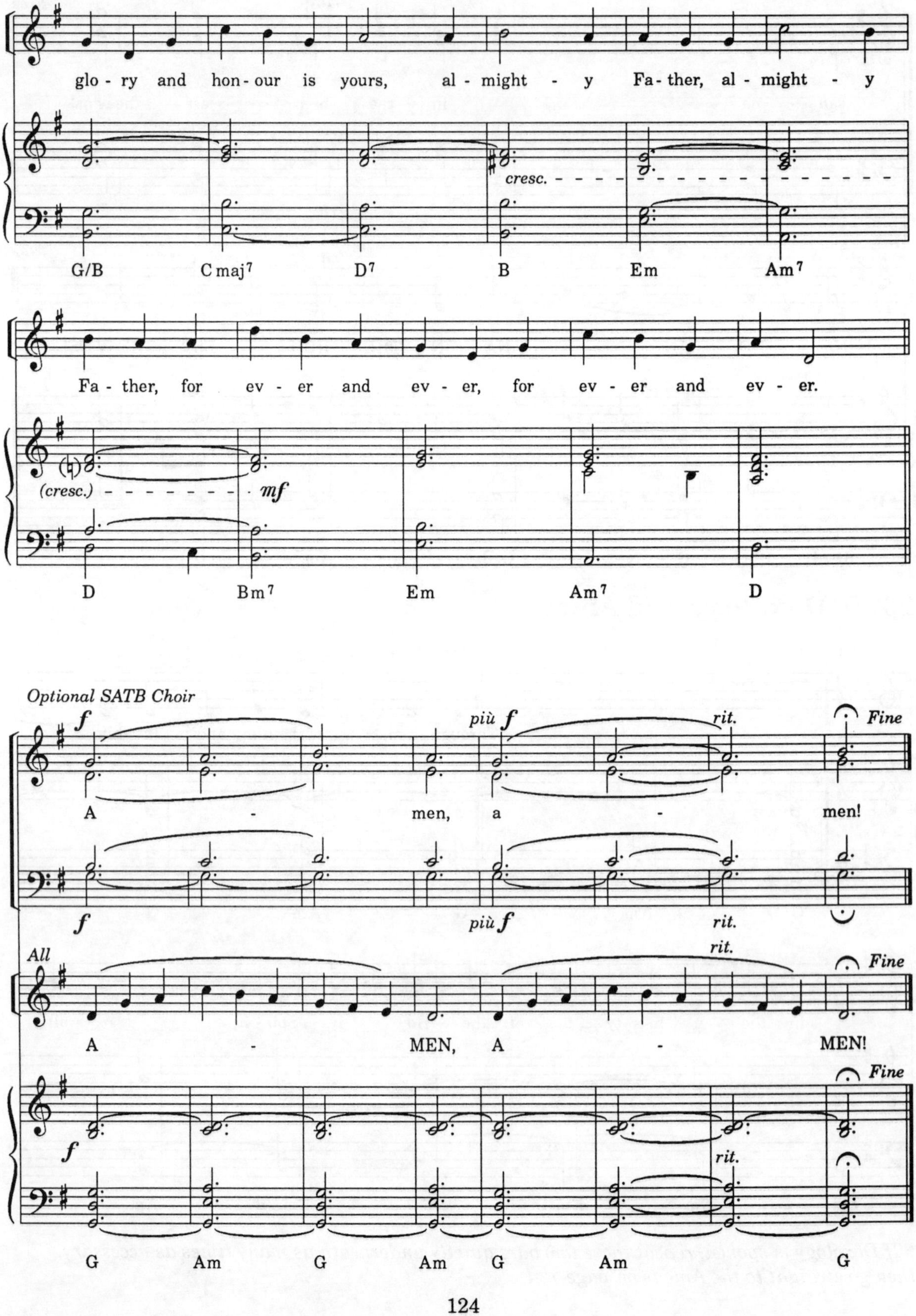
glo - ry and hon - our is yours, al - might - y Fa - ther, al - might - y
cresc.
G/B Cmaj7 D7 B Em Am7
Fa - ther, for ev - er and ev - er, for ev - er and ev - er.
(cresc.) mf
D Bm7 Em Am7 D
Optional SATB Choir
f più f rit. Fine
A - men, a - men!
f più f rit.
All
rit. Fine
A - MEN, A - MEN!
Fine
f rit.
G Am G Am G Am G

208 "Seventy Times Seven" Acclamations

Chris McCurry

208A Holy, holy

(Piano preferred)

HO - LY, HO - LY, HO - LY LORD,

GOD OF POWER AND MIGHT. HEAV'N AND EARTH ARE FULL OF YOUR GLO - RY.

HO - SAN - NA, HO - SAN - NA, HO - SAN - NA IN THE

HIGH - EST. Bless - ed is

125

he who comes, who comes— in the name of the Lord. HO -

Gm (Em)   E♭ (C)   A♭ (F)   Fm (Dm)   G (E)   C (A)

SAN - NA, HO - SAN - NA, HO - SAN - NA IN THE HIGH - EST.

B♭ (G)   Dm (Bm)   A♭ (F)   E♭ (C)   C (A)   F (D)   E♭ (C)   B♭ (G)

208B, C Memorial Acclamations

208B

All

Let us pro-claim the my - ste - ry of faith. CHRIST HAS DIED,

Capo 3 (G)   B♭   G⁹ (E⁹)

Capo 3 (G)

CHRIST IS RIS-EN, CHRIST WILL COME A - GAIN.____ - GAIN.____

1   *2*

C (A)   Em (C#m)   E♭ (C)   Dm⁷ (Bm⁷)   E♭ (C)   F⁷ (D⁷)   G (E)

208C

All

WHEN WE EAT THIS BREAD, WHEN WE DRINK THIS CUP, WE PRO-

Capo 3

B♭	Dm⁷	G^sus	G	C	Em	A	F
(G)	(Bm⁷)	(E^sus)	(E)	(A)	(C#m)	(F#)	(D)

CLAIM YOUR DEATH, LORD_ JE - SUS, UN - TIL YOU COME IN_ GLO - RY.

B♭	Dm	A♭	E♭	C	F	E♭	B♭
(G)	(Bm)	(F)	(C)	(A)	(D)	(C)	(G)

208D Doxology and Great Amen

Through him, with_ him, in_ him, in the u - ni - ty of the Ho — ly Spi - rit, all glo - ry and

ho - nour is yours, al - migh - ty Fa - ther, for e - ver and e - ver. A - MEN,

All

Capo 3 (G) (E⁹)

B♭	G⁹

1. *2.*

A - MEN, A - MEN, A - MEN. -MEN.___

C	Em	E♭	Dm⁷	E♭	F⁷	G
(A)	(C#m)	(C)	(Bm⁷)	(C)	(D⁷)	(E)

127

209 Responsorial Acclamations

Chris McCurry

209A Holy, holy

209B, C Memorial Acclamations

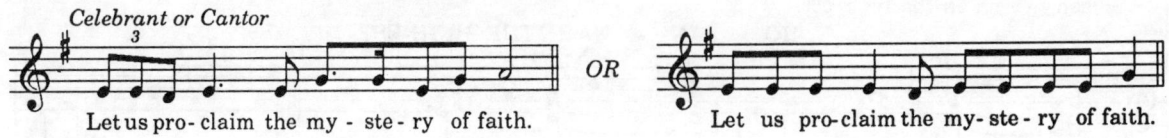

Celebrant or Cantor

Let us pro-claim the my-ste-ry of faith.   OR   Let us pro-claim the my-ste-ry of faith.

209B

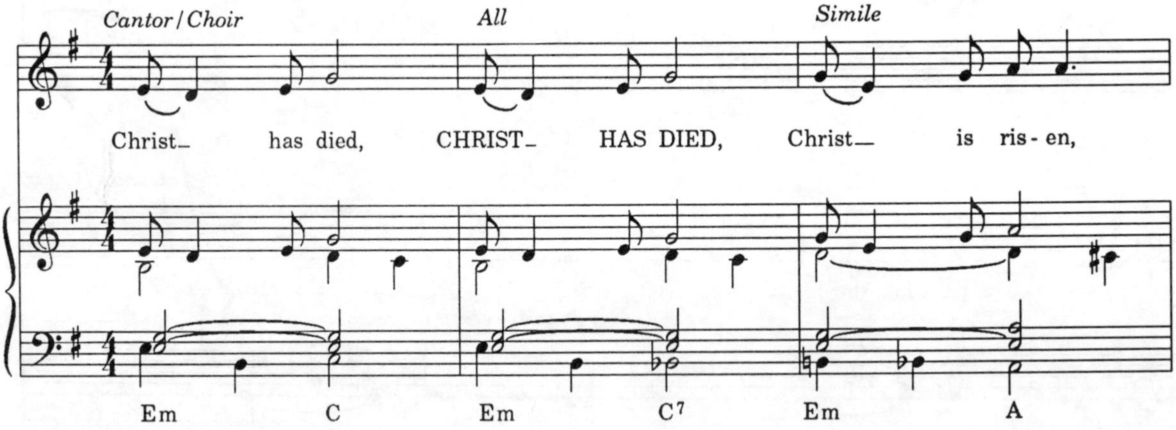

Cantor / Choir   *All*   *Simile*

Christ— has died, CHRIST— HAS DIED, Christ— is ris-en,

Em   C   Em   C^7 Em   A

CHRIST— IS RIS-EN, Christ will come a-gain, CHRIST WILL COME A-GAIN.

Em   A   G   E   G   E

130

209C

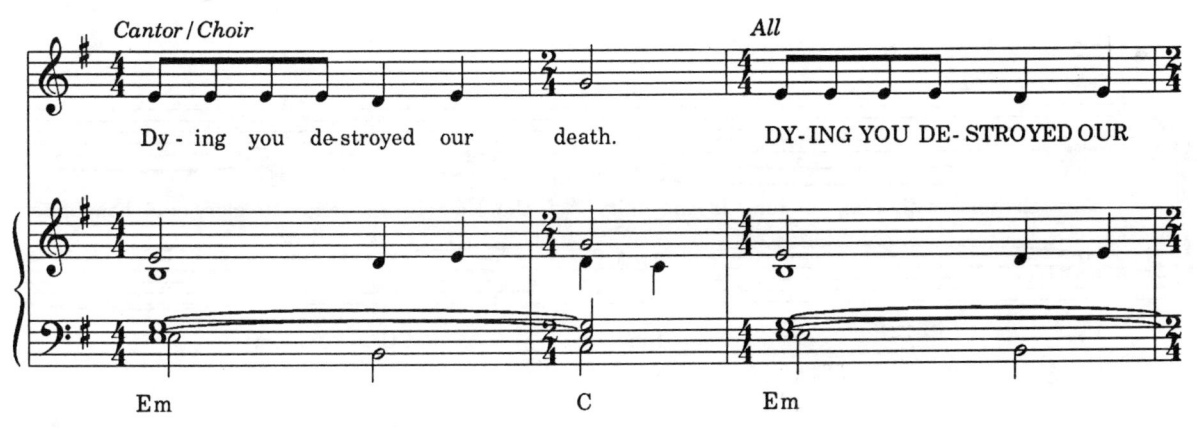

Dy-ing you de-stroyed our death. DY-ING YOU DE-STROYED OUR

Em   C   Em

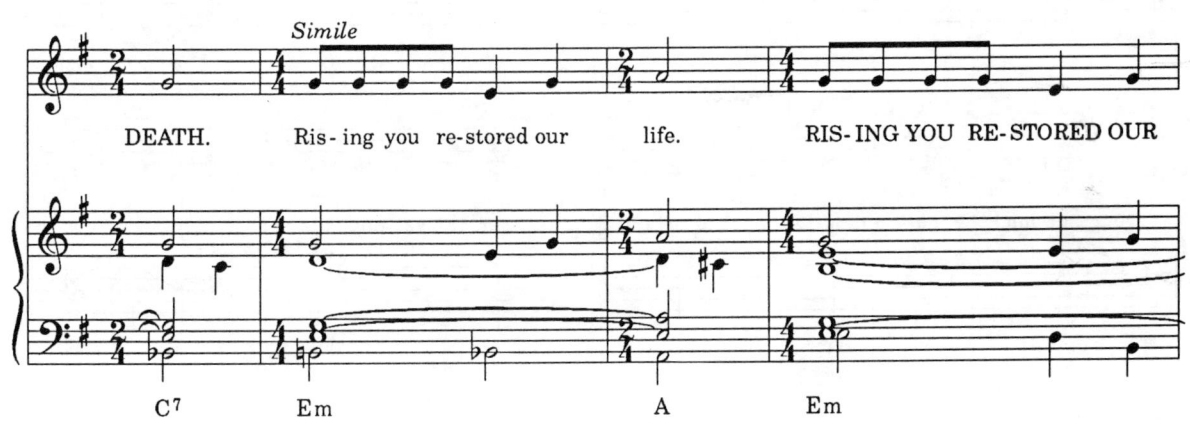

DEATH. Ris-ing you re-stored our life. RIS-ING YOU RE-STORED OUR

C⁷   Em   A   Em

LIFE. Lord Je - sus, come in glo - ry. LORD JE - SUS, COME IN GLO - RY.

A   *N.C.   G   E   N.C.   G   E

*N.C.= No chord

131

209D Doxology and Great Amen

210 Eucharistic Acclamations

Peter McGrail

from Mass of St John of the Cross

210A Holy, holy

SAN - NA, HO - SAN - NA IN THE HIGH - EST.

Bless - ed is he who comes,

who comes in the name of the Lord.

WHO COMES IN THE

NAME OF THE LORD. Ho - san - na, ho - san - na in the high - est.

HO -

SAN - NA, HO - SAN - NA IN THE HIGH - EST.

134

210B Memorial Acclamation A

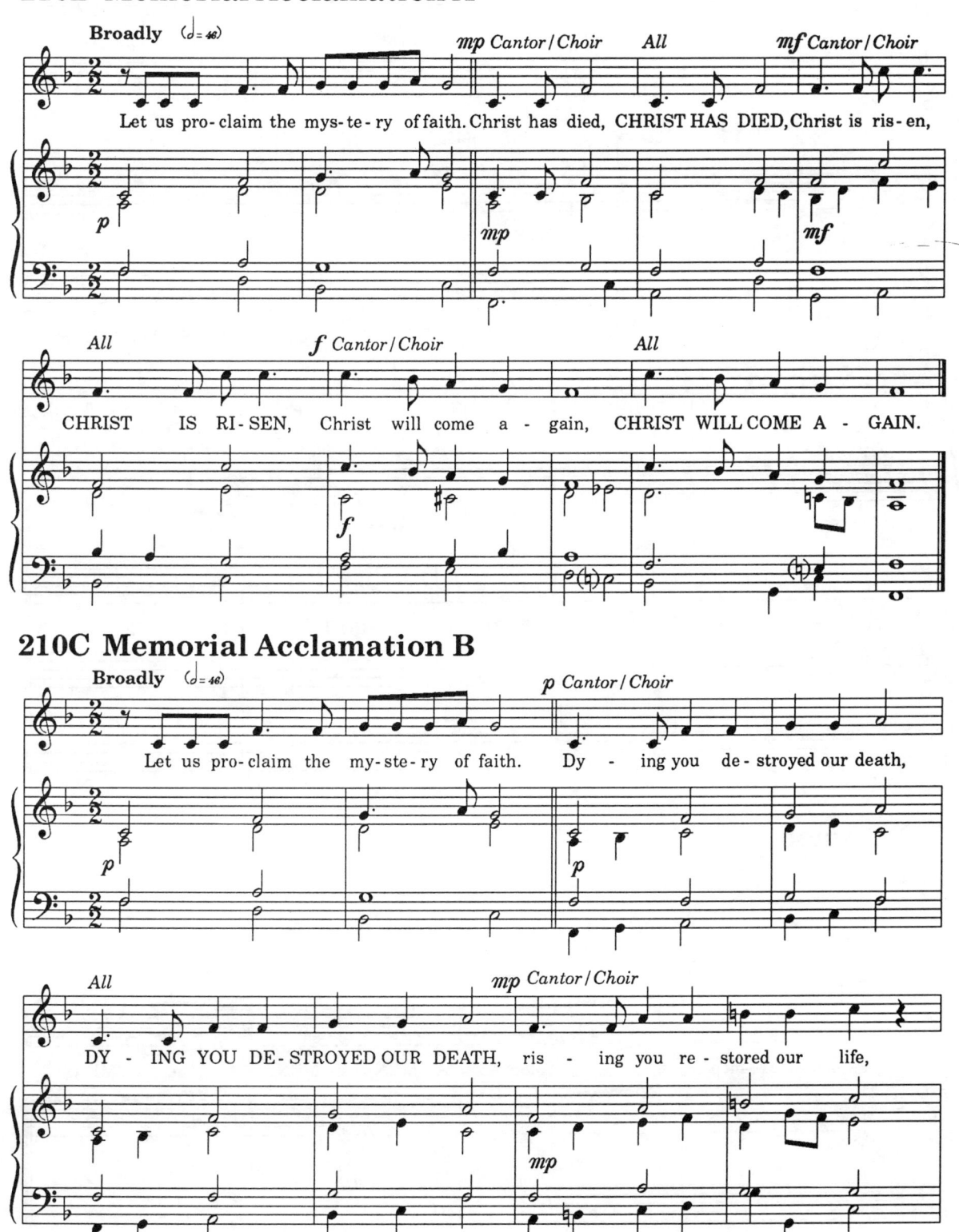

Broadly (♩= 46)

mp Cantor / Choir   All   *mf* Cantor / Choir

Let us pro-claim the mys-te-ry of faith. Christ has died, CHRIST HAS DIED, Christ is ris-en,

All   *f* Cantor / Choir   *All*

CHRIST   IS RI-SEN,   Christ will come a-gain, CHRIST WILL COME A - GAIN.

210C Memorial Acclamation B

Broadly (♩= 46)

p Cantor / Choir

Let us pro-claim the my-ste-ry of faith. Dy - ing you de-stroyed our death,

All   *mp* Cantor / Choir

DY - ING YOU DE-STROYED OUR DEATH, ris - ing you re-stored our   life,

135

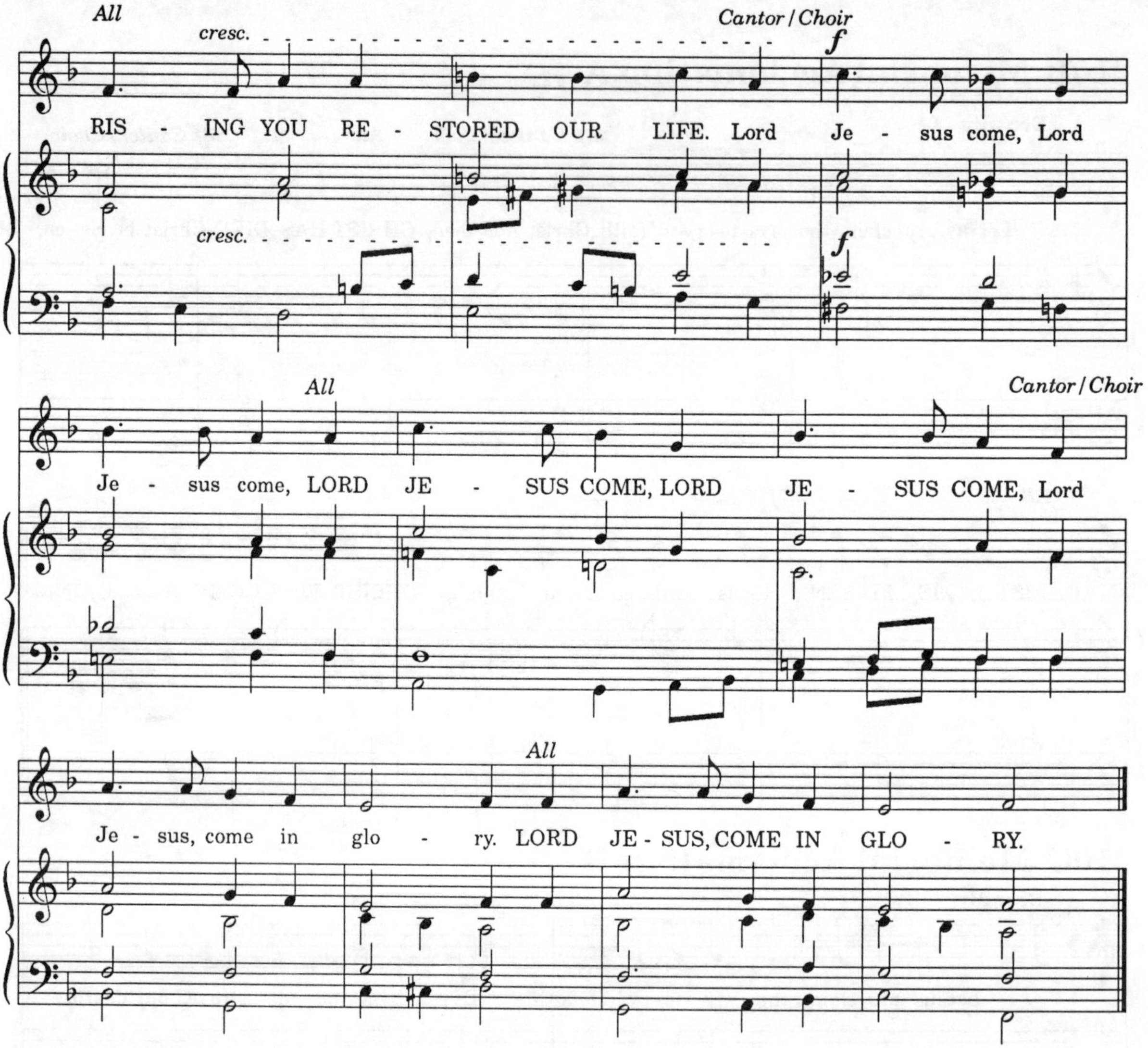
All
cresc.
Cantor / Choir
f
RIS - ING YOU RE - STORED OUR LIFE. Lord Je - sus come, Lord
cresc.
f
All
Cantor / Choir
Je - sus come, LORD JE - SUS COME, LORD JE - SUS COME, Lord
All
Je - sus, come in glo - ry. LORD JE - SUS, COME IN GLO - RY.

210D Amen

Celebrant
. . . for e - ver and e - ver.

Celebrant uses Missal Tone, starting on 'A'.

f Cantor / Choir
All
A - men, a - men, a - men. A - MEN, A - MEN, A - MEN.
f

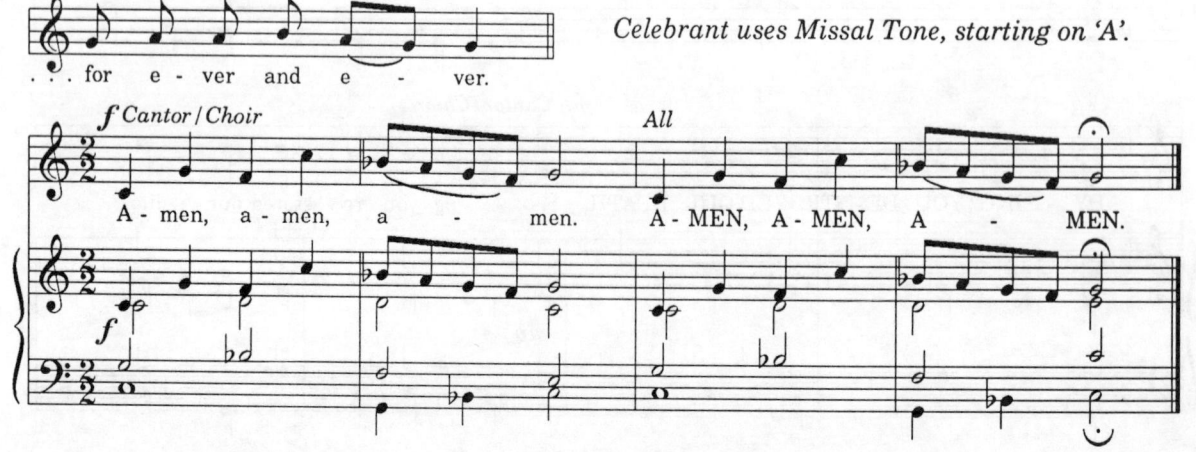

211 Holy, holy

Fintan P O'Carroll

from Mass of the Immaculate Conception

212 Memorial Acclamation and Great Amen

Fintan P O'Carroll

from Mass of the Annunciation

212A Memorial Acclamation

People **Molto sostenuto**

WHEN WE EAT THIS BREAD AND DRINK THIS CUP, WE PRO-

Choir **Molto sostenuto**

When we eat this bread and drink this cup, we pro-

CLAIM YOUR DEATH, LORD JE - SUS, UN-TIL YOU COME IN GLO - RY.

claim your death, Lord Je - sus, un-til you come in glo - ry.

212B Great Amen

Maestoso (♩ = 84)

A - - - men, a - - - men,

a - - - men, a - - - men.

213 Carnival Sanctus

Chris O'Hara

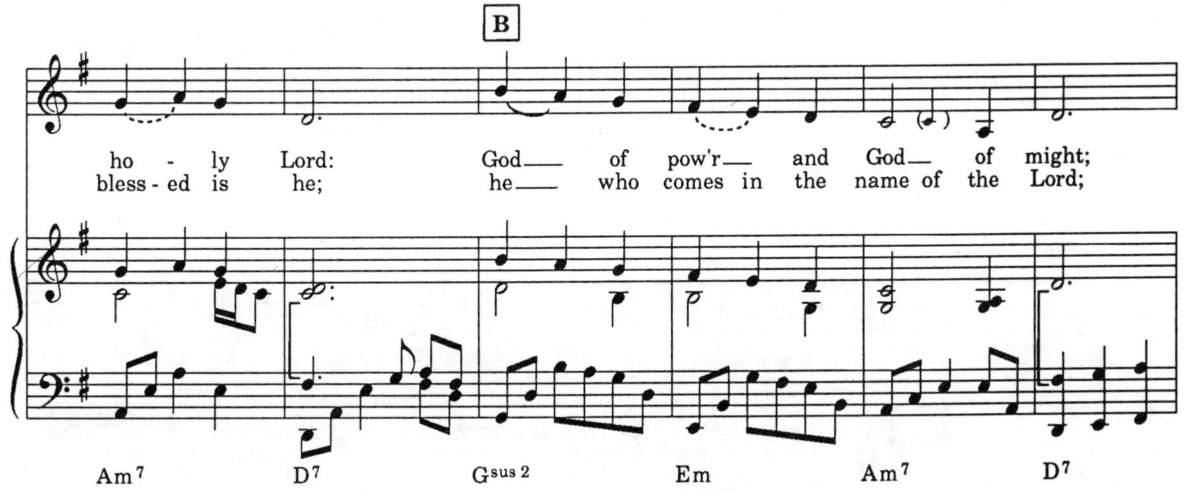

(♩ = 73)

% A

(Intro.)

1. Ho - ly,   ho - ly,
2. Bless - ed,   bless - ed,

G sus 2   Em

B

ho - ly Lord: God— of pow'r— and God— of might;
bless - ed is he;   he— who comes in the name of the Lord;

Am⁷   D⁷   G sus 2   Em   Am⁷   D⁷

This piece may be sung in unison throughout, or as a three-part canon, the voices entering at four-bar intervals at A, B and C.

Heav-en and earth— are full of your glory, Ho - san-na!_____ Ho -

Gsus 2   Em   Am7   D7   Gsus 2   Em

san-na!_____ Ho - san - na in— the high-est!_____

Am7   D7   Gsus 2   Em   Am7   D7   G

214 Holy, holy

House of the Open Door Community

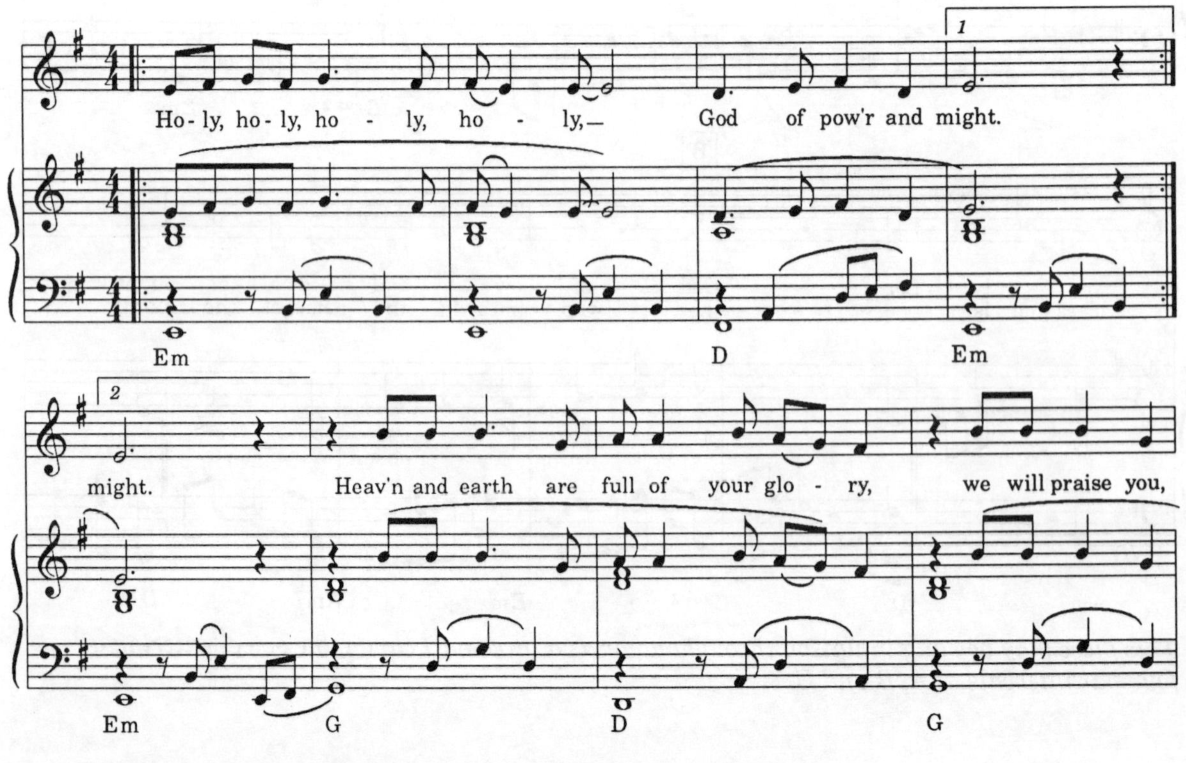

Ho - ly, ho - ly, ho - ly, ho - ly,— God of pow'r and might.

Em   D   Em

might. Heav'n and earth are full of your glo - ry, we will praise you,

Em   G   D   G

140

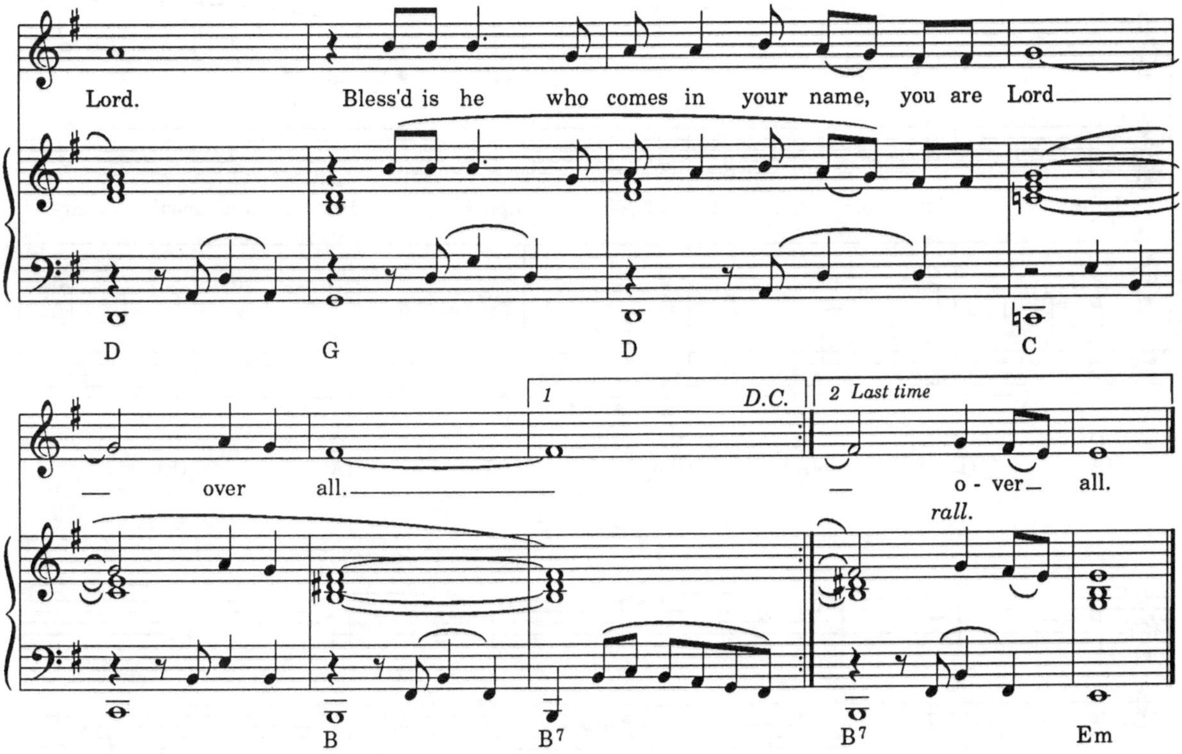

Lord. Bless'd is he who comes in your name, you are Lord
D G D C
1 D.C.
2 Last time
over all.
o - ver all.
rall.
B B7 B7 Em

215 Eucharistic Acclamations 1

Bernard Sexton

215A Holy, holy

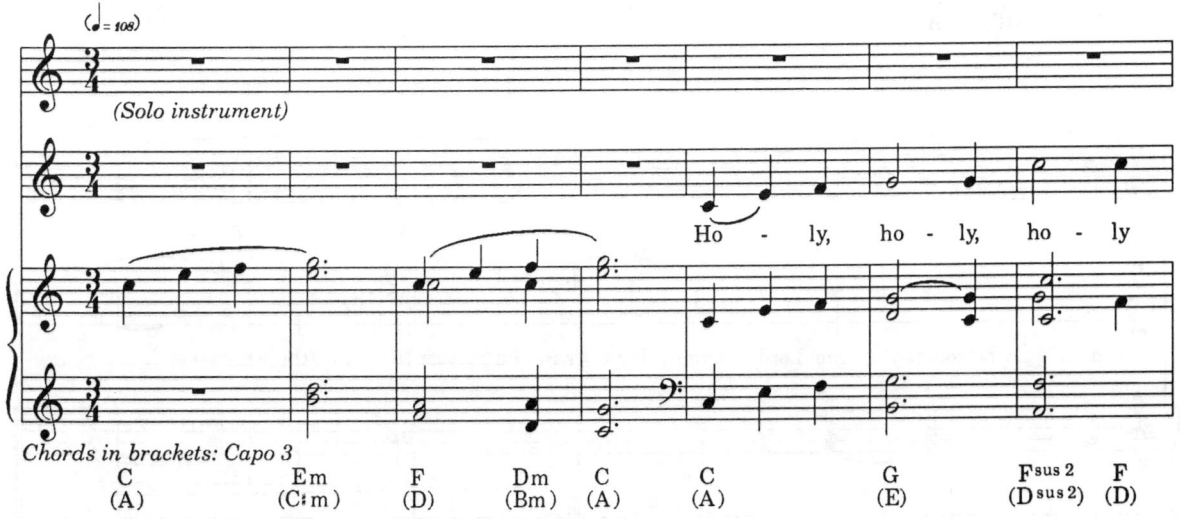

(♩= 108)
(Solo instrument)
Ho - ly, ho - ly, ho - ly
Chords in brackets: Capo 3
C (A) Em (C♯m) F (D) Dm (Bm) C (A) C (A) G (E) Fsus 2 (Dsus 2) F (D)

* *Guitar chords are an alternative to the keyboard accompaniment.*

215B Memorial Acclamation

215C Great Amen

216 Our Father

Fintan P O'Carroll

from Mass of the Immaculate Conception

Andante tranquillo

All (unison)

Our— Fa - ther, who art— in— hea - ven, hal - lowed be thy—

name. Thy— king - dom come, thy will be done on earth as it is in—

hea - ven. Give— us this day our dai - ly bread, and for - give us— our—

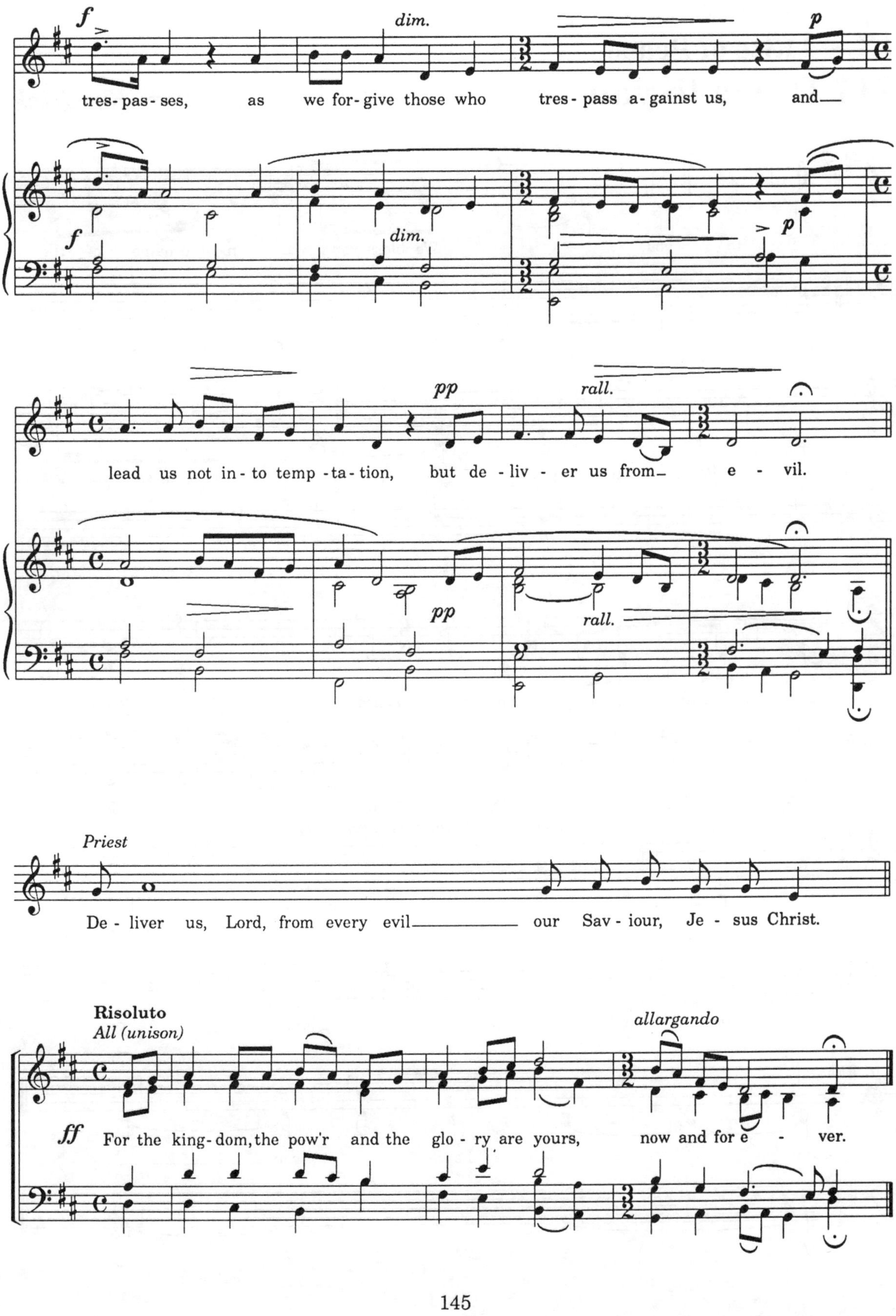

trespasses, as we forgive those who trespass against us, and

lead us not into temptation, but deliver us from evil.

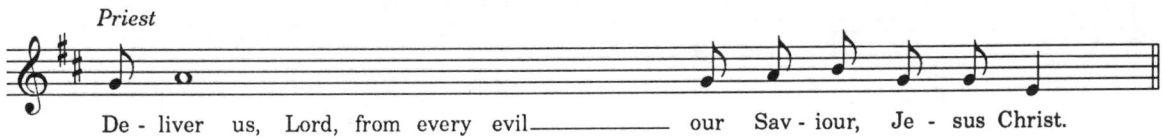

Priest

Deliver us, Lord, from every evil our Saviour, Jesus Christ.

Risoluto
All (unison)

allargando

ff For the kingdom, the pow'r and the glory are yours, now and for ever.

217 Peace to you

Graham Kendrick

218 Lamb of God

Geoffrey Boulton Smith

from Mass in Folk Style

219 Lamb of God

from Mass of St Edmund of Abingdon

Derek Fry

Lamb of God, you take a-way the sins of the world: have mer-cy on us. Lamb of God, you take a-way the sins of the world: have mer-cy on us. Lamb of God, you take a-way the sins of the

220 Lamb of God

Patrick Geary

for Clifton Diocese Primary School Leavers' Mass

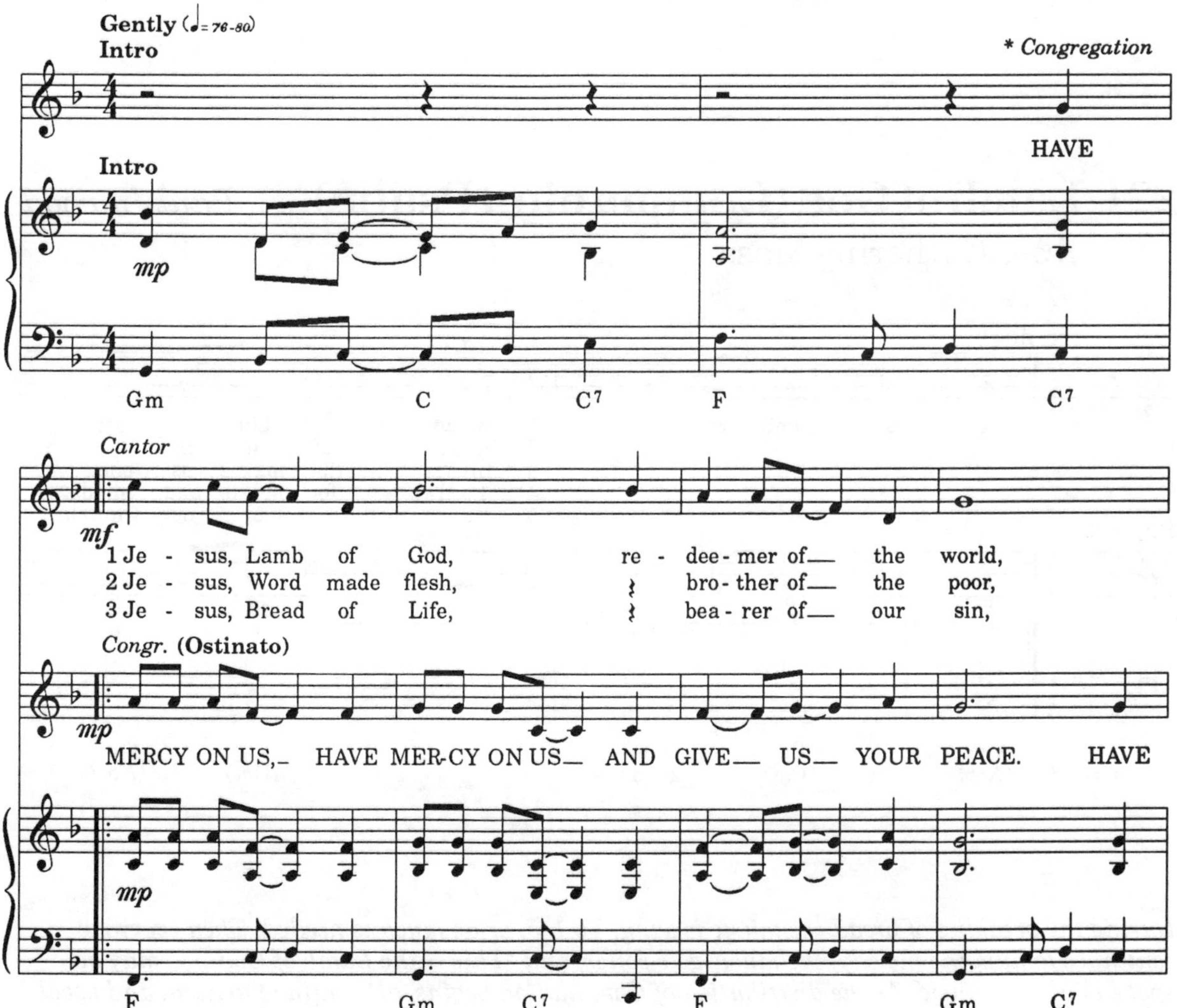

* The Ostinato should be sung through once by all before the Cantor starts the verses.

Je - sus, Lamb of God,
Je - sus, Word made flesh,
Je - sus, Bread of Life,
} Give— us— your peace.

MER-CY ON US,— HAVE MERCY ON US— AND GIVE— US— YOUR PEACE. HAVE

F   Gm   C⁷   Gm   C⁷   F   C⁷

221 Lamb of God (Communion Psalm) *Paul Inwood*

from Gathering Mass

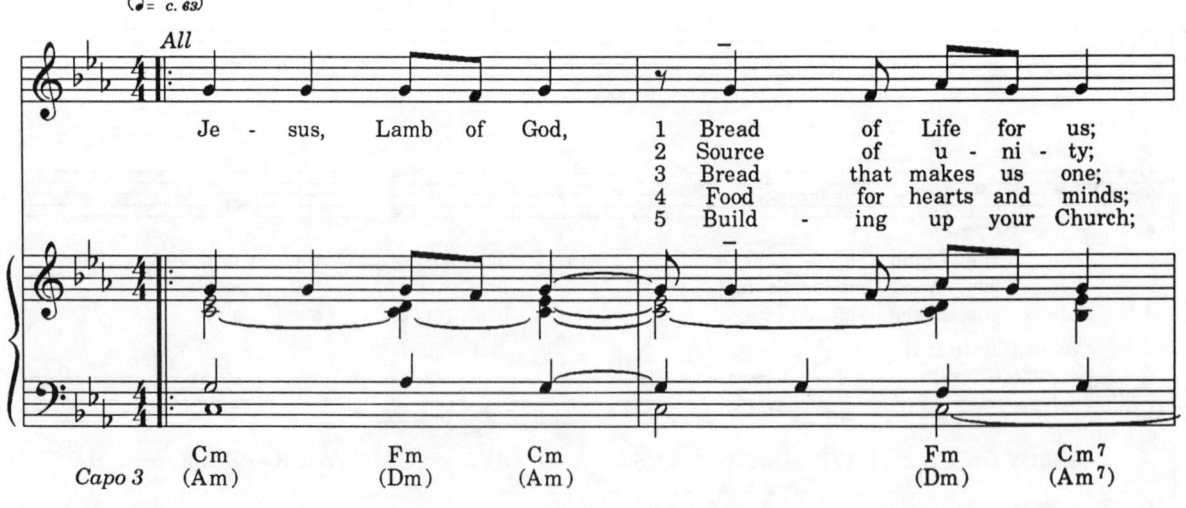

All

Je - sus,   Lamb   of   God,

1   Bread   of   Life   for   us;
2   Source   of   u - ni - ty;
3   Bread   that makes us   one;
4   Food   for   hearts and   minds;
5   Build - ing   up   your   Church;

Capo 3   Cm   Fm   Cm   Fm   Cm⁷
         (Am)   (Dm)   (Am)   (Dm)   (Am⁷)

During the breaking of bread the music is sung, Vs 1–5, or as much is needed. Then everyone continues to hum the melody, the music gets softer, and "This is the Lamb of God … " may be spoken over the music. As the distribution of Communion begins, all continue to hum, and vocal or instrumental descants are added ad lib.

Further verses and instrumental descants can be found in the version of this Mass published by OCP.

* ⌢ *last time only*

222 Lamb of God

Peter Jones

Lamb— of God, you take a-way the sins of the world:_____ have mer-cy on us. HAVE MER-CY ON US.

Lamb— of God, you take a-way the sins of the world:_____ have mer-cy on us. HAVE MER-CY ON US.

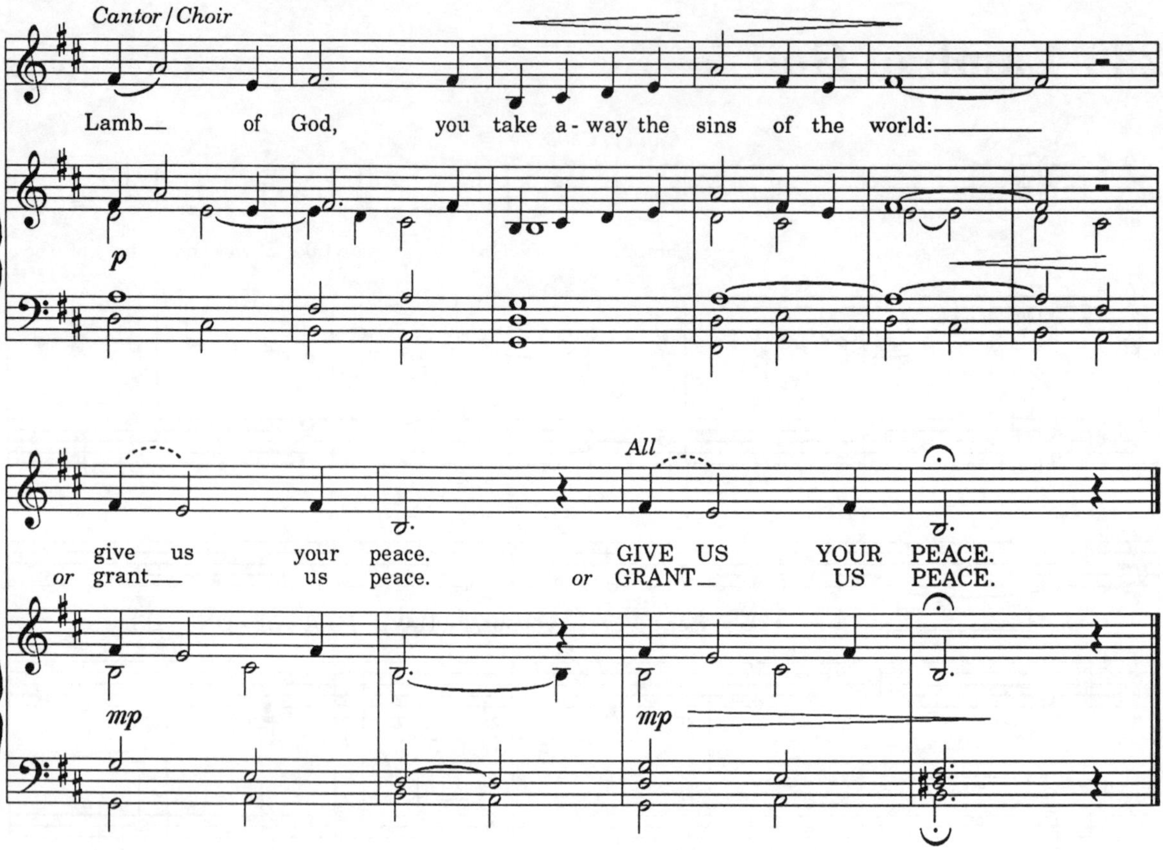
Cantor / Choir
Lamb of God, you take a-way the sins of the world:
p
give us your peace.
or grant us peace.
All
GIVE US YOUR PEACE.
or GRANT US PEACE.
mp
mp

223 Lamb of God

from Mass of St George

Shaun MacCarthy

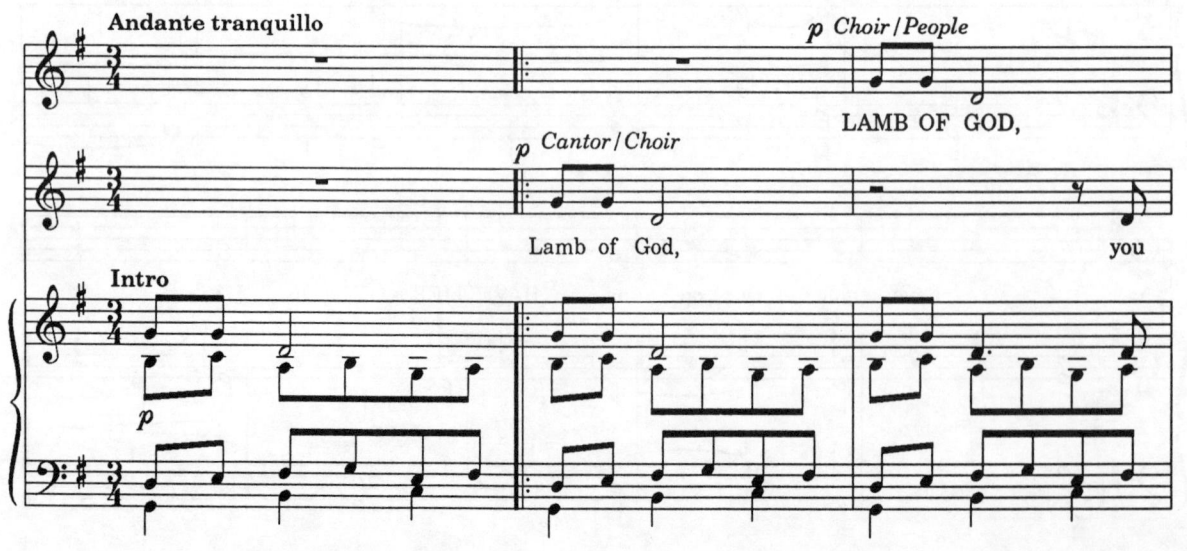

Andante tranquillo
p Choir / People
LAMB OF GOD,
p Cantor / Choir
Lamb of God, you
Intro
p

TAKE A - WAY THE SINS OF THE WORLD: GRANT US PEACE.

world: grant us peace.

224 Peace Song/Agnus Dei

Peter McGrail

Largo (♩ = 60)

mp

G   Em   Am   D

Cantor / Choir   *All*

Lo - ving Sa - viour, bread of life: COME AND BRING YOUR PEACE.

G   Em   Am   Dsus 4   D

157

2	*Cantor/Choir*	:	Lord who calmed the stormy seas,
	All	:	COME AND BRING YOUR PEACE.
	Cantor/Choir	:	Lord, you hear the ones who call,
	All	:	COME AND BRING YOUR PEACE.
		:	JESUS, LORD, BE MERCIFUL TO US,
		:	JESUS, LAMB OF GOD, FILL US WITH YOUR LOVE.

3	*Cantor/Choir*	:	To our homes and families,
	All	:	COME AND BRING YOUR PEACE.
	Cantor/Choir	:	To our friends and dear ones,
	All	:	COME AND BRING YOUR PEACE.
		:	JESUS, LORD, BE MERCIFUL TO US,
		:	JESUS, LAMB OF GOD, FILL US WITH YOUR LOVE.

4	*Cantor/Choir*	:	Lord, you know our deepest needs,
	All	:	COME AND BRING YOUR PEACE.
	Cantor/Choir	:	Lord, you hear our darkest fears,
	All	:	COME AND BRING YOUR PEACE.
		:	JESUS, LORD, BE MERCIFUL TO US,
		:	JESUS, LAMB OF GOD, FILL US WITH YOUR LOVE.

5	*Cantor/Choir*	:	Show to us your tenderness,
	All	:	COME AND BRING YOUR PEACE.
	Cantor/Choir	:	Heal us with your gentle love,
	All	:	COME AND BRING YOUR PEACE.
		:	JESUS, LORD BE MERCIFUL TO US,
		:	JESUS, LAMB OF GOD, FILL US WITH YOUR LOVE.

225 Bread of the world

Words: Bishop Reginald Heber
Music: John Ainslie

Bread of the world in mer - cy bro - ken, wine of the soul in mer - cy shed, by whom the words of life were spo - ken, and in whose death our sins____ are dead. Look on the heart by sor - row bro - ken,

look on the tears by sin - ners shed; and be your feast to us the to - ken that by your grace our souls are fed.

226 In Praise of Christ

Words: Patrick Lee
Music: Geoffrey Boulton Smith

Christ, you are the Light which points the way. Christ, you are the Way which leads to truth. Christ, you are the Truth which brings us

This piece will most frequently be sung by a soloist or choir in unison with organ accompaniment, though it could be sung by All. The text could also be divided between different singers, or the piece could even be attempted SATB, with basses going up to D at the last chord.

life. Christ, you are the Life which con - quers death.

Praise— our Light, praise— our Way, our Truth, our Life. Christ be our Light.

Christ be our Way. Christ be our Truth. Christ be our Life. Christ— be All.

Christ— be All. Christ be our Life.——— Christ— be All.

If desired the piece may end here, with ♩ in all parts.

227 Your love is finer than life (Psalm 62(63))

Marty Haugen

Introduction Simply (♩ = 80-84)
Woodwinds in C

mf

Refrain
2nd, 3rd and last time

℁

➤ *p* (a tempo) *mp*

Descant ℁ *mp* (a tempo)

Oh- God, I seek You, my soul thirsts for You, Your love is—

Choir/Assembly - Melody ℁ *mf* (a tempo)

Oh God, I seek You, my soul thirsts for You, Your love is

℁ (a tempo)

mf

Capo 2 | F♯m (Em) | C♯m⁷ (Bm⁷) | F♯m E/G♯ (Em)(D/F♯) | A (G) | Bm (Am) | D (C)

1,2,3 to Verses | *Last time*

mp *dim.* *rit.* *rit.* *p*

fin-er than life.____ fin-er, Your love is__ fin-er than life.
rit.

fin-er than life.____ fin-er than life.____

1,2,3 to Verses | *Last time*

rit.

E (D) | F♯ 4-3 (E⁴⁻³) | F♯ (E) | E (D) | D (C) | E (D) | F♯ (E)

Verses

Vs 1 and 3 only

mf 1 As a dry and wear - y des - ert land, so my

p 2 I think on You when at night I rest, I re -
f 3 I will bless Your name all the days I live, I will

F♯m⁷
(Em⁷)

B⁷/F♯
(A⁷/E)

soul is thirst-ing for my God, and my flesh is faint for the

flect u - pon Your stead - fast love. I will cling to You, Oh
raise my hands and call on You. My joy - ful lips shall

B m⁷/F♯
(Am⁷/E)

C♯m⁷
(Bm⁷)

F♯
(E)

F♯m⁷
(Em⁷)

163

1 & 2

rit.   D.S. (to refrain)

rit.   D.S. (to refrain)

God I seek, for Your love is more to me than life._____

rit.   D.S. (to refrain)

Lord my God, in the shad-ow of Your wings I sing._____
sing Your praise, You a-lone have filled my hun-gry soul._____

rit.   D.S. (to refrain)

rit.

B⁷/F♯   Bm/D   G♯m⁷(♭5)   Bm/C♯   C♯⁷
(A⁷/E)   (Am/C)   (F♯m⁷(♭5))   (Am/B)   (B⁷)

228 As the deer longs (Psalm 42(43))

for Marty Haugen

Bob Hurd
Arr. Craig S. Kingsbury

Intro

mp

Dm   Dm/C   B♭maj⁷   Am   F   Am⁷

B♭maj⁷   Dsus4   Dm   Gm⁷   Am⁷   Dm   C/D   B♭/D   Am⁷/D

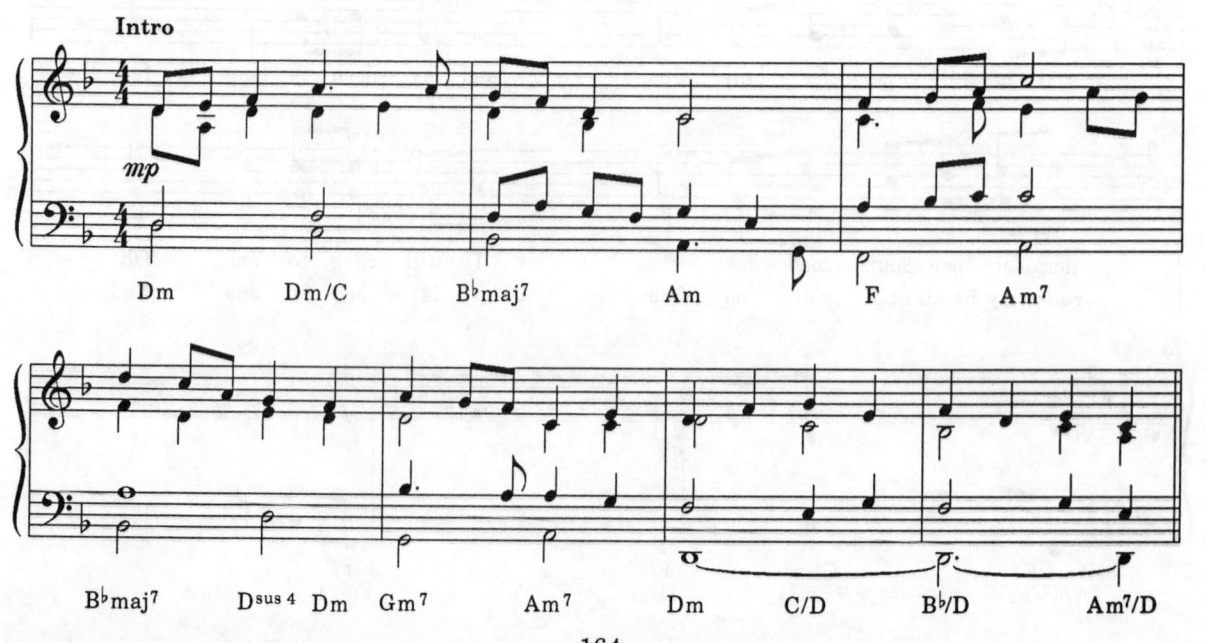

164

As the deer longs for run - ning streams, so I___ long,

so I___ long,___ so I___ long for you.___

1-5 to Verses | Final | Fine

ritard.

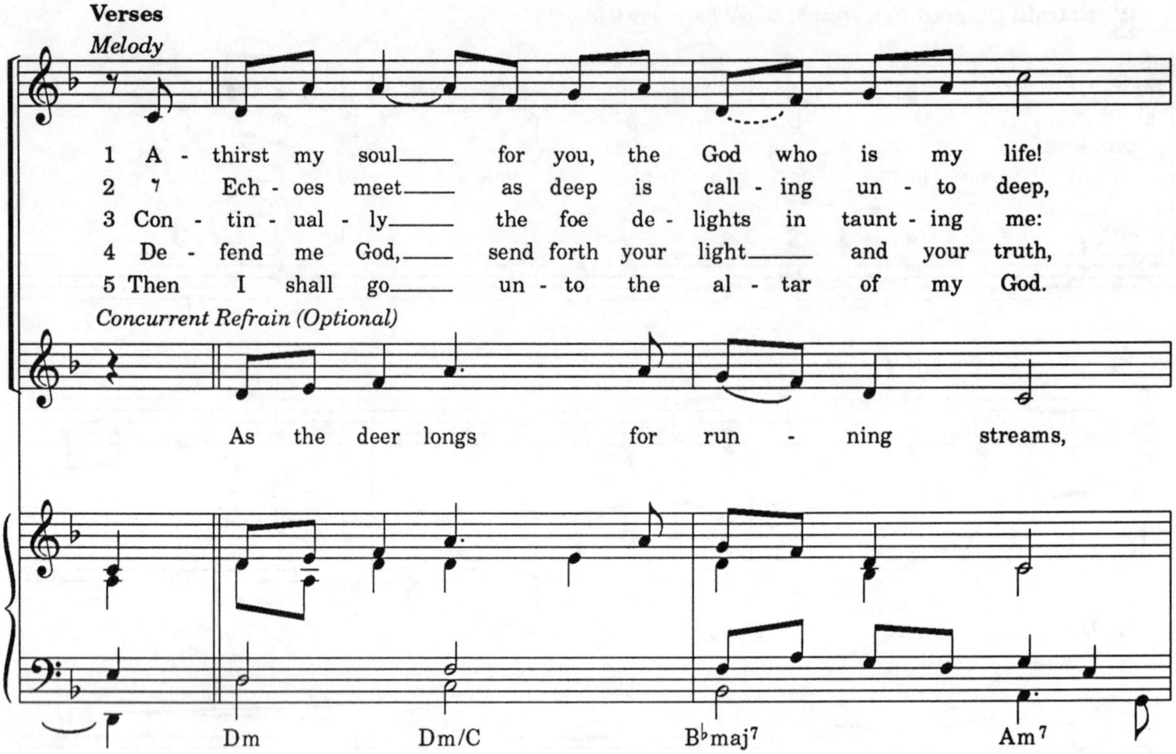

Verses

Melody

1 A - thirst my soul___ for you, the God who is my life!
2 ⁊ Ech - oes meet___ as deep is call - ing un - to deep,
3 Con - tin - ual - ly___ the foe de - lights in taunt - ing me:
4 De - fend me God,___ send forth your light___ and your truth,
5 Then I shall go___ un - to the al - tar of my God.

Concurrent Refrain (Optional)

As the deer longs for run - ning streams,

Dm   Dm/C   B♭maj⁷   Am⁷

At V3, Refrain and Verse may be sung together.

When shall I see, when shall I___ see,___
o - ver my head, all your might - y wa - ters,
"Where is God,___ where is your___ God?"___
they will lead me to your ho - ly moun - tain,
Prais - ing you,___ O my joy and glad - ness:

so I___ long, so I___ long,___

F   Am⁷   B♭maj⁷   Dsus 4   Dm

166

see   the face   of   God?_____
sweep - ing o   - ver me._____
Where,   O where   are you?_____
to   your dwell - ing place._____
I   shall praise your name._____

so I____ long for you._____

Gm⁷   Am⁷   Dm   C/D   B♭/D   Am/D

D.S.
D.S.
D.S.

Craig S. Kingsbury

Solo instrument
Intro

℅ **Refrain**

| 1-5 | | Final | *Fine* | **Verses**

ritard.

D.S.

167

229 O Lord, Your tenderness

Graham Kendrick

James 5:11

With feeling

O Lord, Your tend-er-ness,— melt-ing all my bit-ter-ness, O Lord, I re-ceive Your love.—

— O Lord, Your love-li-ness,— chang-ing all my ug-li-ness,— O Lord, I re-ceive Your love.

— O— Lord, I re-ceive Your love,—

O— Lord, I re- ceive Your— love.———

230 Ubi Caritas

Chris McCurry

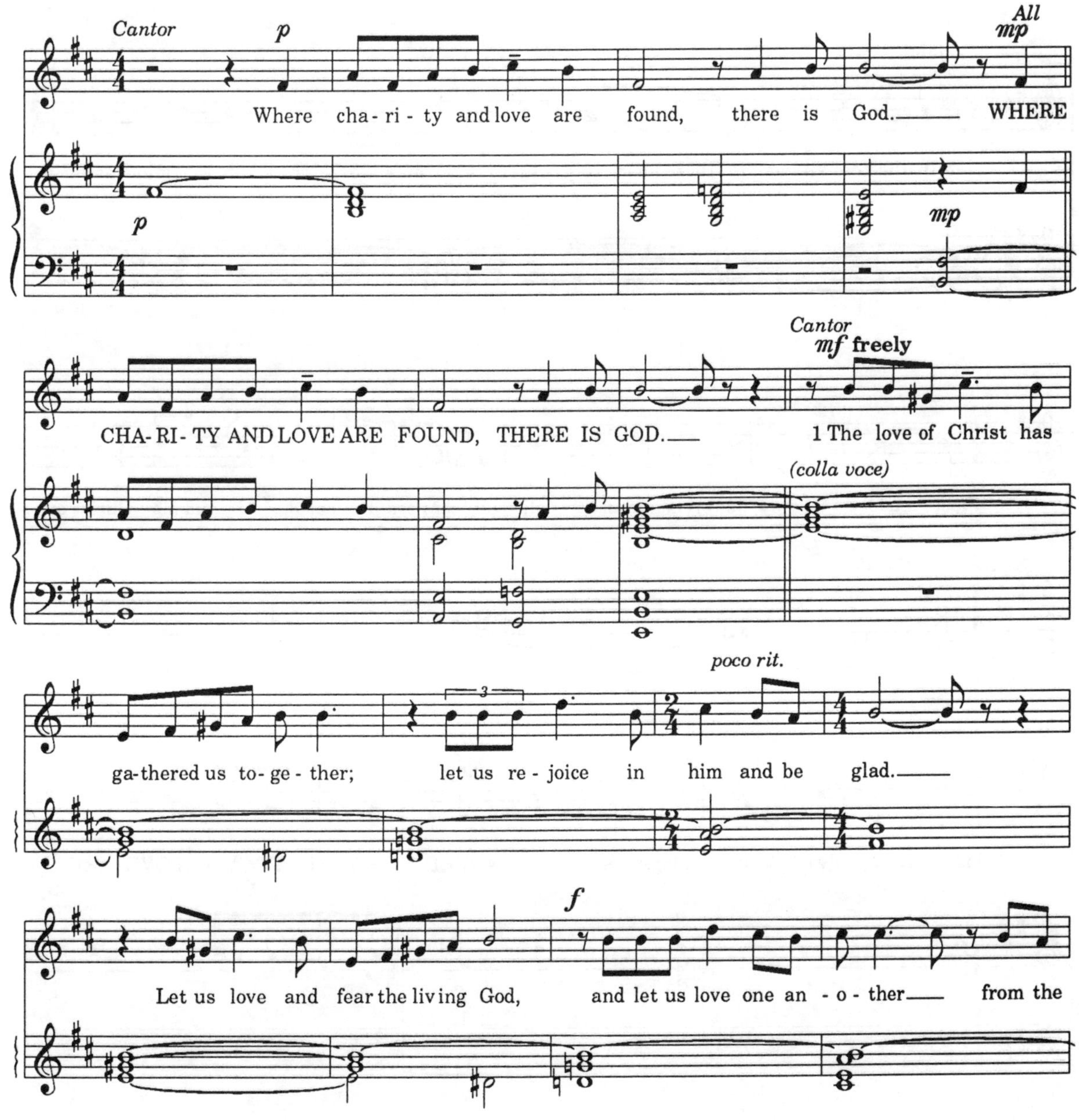

Cantor *p* *All* *mp*

Where cha- ri- ty and love are found, there is God.—— WHERE

p *mp*

Cantor *mf* freely

CHA- RI- TY AND LOVE ARE FOUND, THERE IS GOD.— 1 The love of Christ has

(colla voce)

poco rit.

ga- thered us to- ge- ther; let us re- joice in him and be glad.——

f

Let us love and fear the liv ing God, and let us love one an- o- ther—— from the

heart.—— WHERE CHA-RI-TY AND LOVE ARE FOUND, THERE IS GOD.——

2 In the Lord's name ga-thered here to-ge-ther, may we be one in mind and

heart;—— may quar-rels cease, all bit-ter-ness be healed,—— and may Christ our

God—— dwell a-mongst us. WHERE CHA-RI-TY AND LOVE ARE

FOUND, THERE IS GOD.___ *Cantor* 3 Grant us, we pray,— that

with the saints in glo-ry we may see your face, O Christ our God;___

there shall we know a great and per-fect joy___ for all e-ter-ni-ty. A-men.

All mp WHERE CHA-RI-TY AND LOVE ARE FOUND, THERE IS GOD.

231 Because the Lord is my shepherd (Psalm 22(23)) *Christopher Walker*

Intro (♩. = c. 46)

%Verses

1 Be - cause the Lord is my
2 ⁊ when the road leads to
3 ⁊ love you make me a
4 ⁊ good - ness al - ways is

shep - herd,_____ I have ev' - ry - thing_____ I need. He lets me
dark - ness,_____ I shall walk there_____ un - a - fraid. E - ven when
ban - quet_____ for my en - e - mies_____ to see. You make me
with me_____ and your mer - cy_____ I know. Your lov - ing

rest in the mead - ow and leads me_____ to the
death is close_____ I have cour - age_____ for your
wel - come,_____ pour - ing down hon - our_____ from your
kind - ness_____ strength - ens me al - ways_____ as I

Capo 1 D   G   A   D

Em/D   D   Em/D

F#m   G   D/F#

172

qui - et streams.
help is there.
might - y hand;
go through life.

He re - stores my soul and he
You are close be - side me with
and this joy fills me with
I shall dwell in your pres - ence for -

Em   A sus 4   A   D   G

Refrain
(All)

leads me in the paths that are right:
com - fort, you are guid - ing my way:
glad - ness, it is too much to bear:
ev - er, giv - ing praise to your name:

Lord, you are my shep - herd,

D⁹   Em   A   D   Em/D

you are my friend. I want to fol - low you al - ways just to

D   A   Bm   F♯m/A   G   D/F♯   Bm

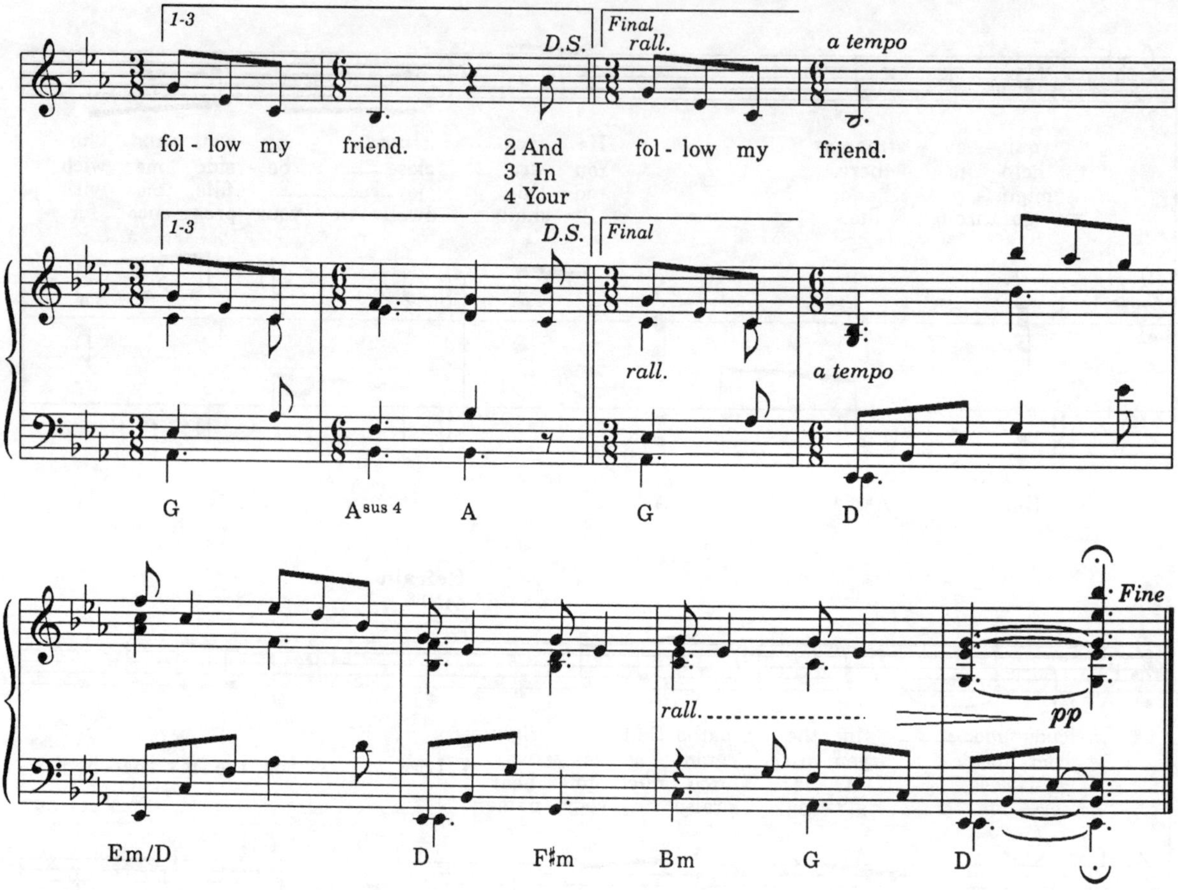
1-3
D.S.
Final
rall.
a tempo
fol - low my friend.
2 And
3 In
4 Your
fol - low my friend.
1-3
D.S.
Final
rall.
a tempo
G
Asus 4
A
G
D
Fine
rall.
pp
Em/D
D
F♯m
Bm
G
D

Solo instrument
Intro (♩. = c. 46)
Verses
Refrain
2
1-3
D.S.
Final
Fine
rall.

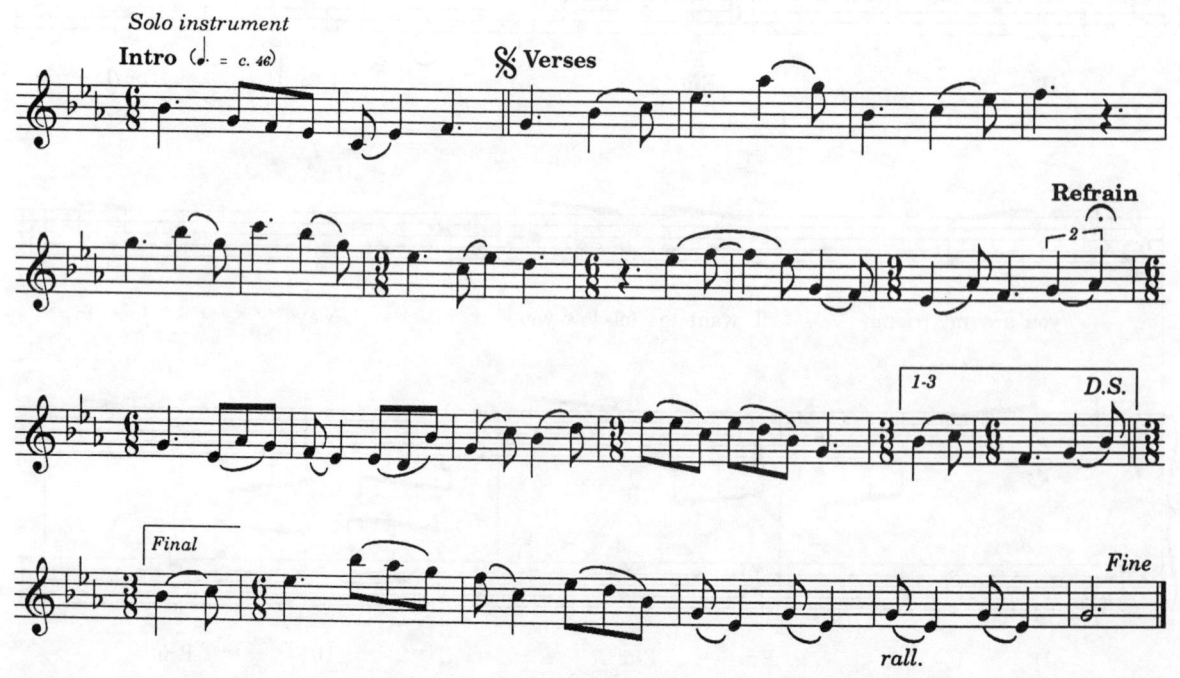

Part IV · Concluding Rite —
Recessional Songs

232 Hymn for Christian Unity

Harold Barker

With breadth

1 Filled with the Spir-it's power, with one acc-ord the in-fant Church con-fessed its ris-en Lord. O Ho-ly Spir-it in the Church to-day no less your pow'r of fell-ow-ship dis-play. Christ-ians prove.

Vs 1 and 2   *(Org.)*   V3   *Fine*

2 Now with the mind of Christ set us on fire
That unity may be our great desire.
Give joy and peace; give faith to hear your call,
And readiness in each to work for all.

3 Widen our love, good Spirit, to embrace
In your strong care the men of every race.
Like wind and fire with life among us move,
Till we are known as Christ's, and Christians prove.

175

233 Go now

Emmanuel Gribben

176

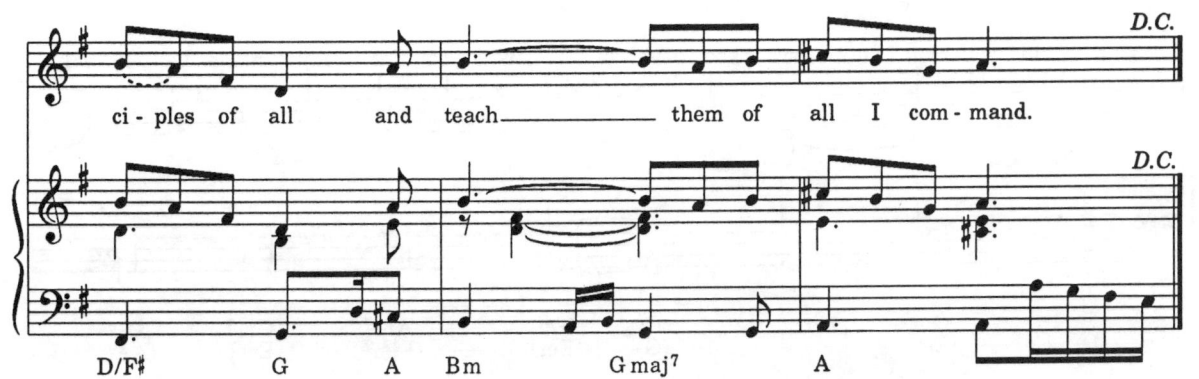

ci - ples of all and teach_____ them of all I com - mand.

D/F♯   G   A   Bm   Gmaj⁷   A

2   I pray that you will be one,
The world must come to believe.
Go, preach forgiveness to all,
Proclaim to the nations my love.

3   Now that my hour has come
And I must leave this world.
Joy is my gift to you,
A joy that the world cannot give.

234 The Summons

Text: The Iona Community
*Tune: **Kelvingrove** (Scottish trad.)*

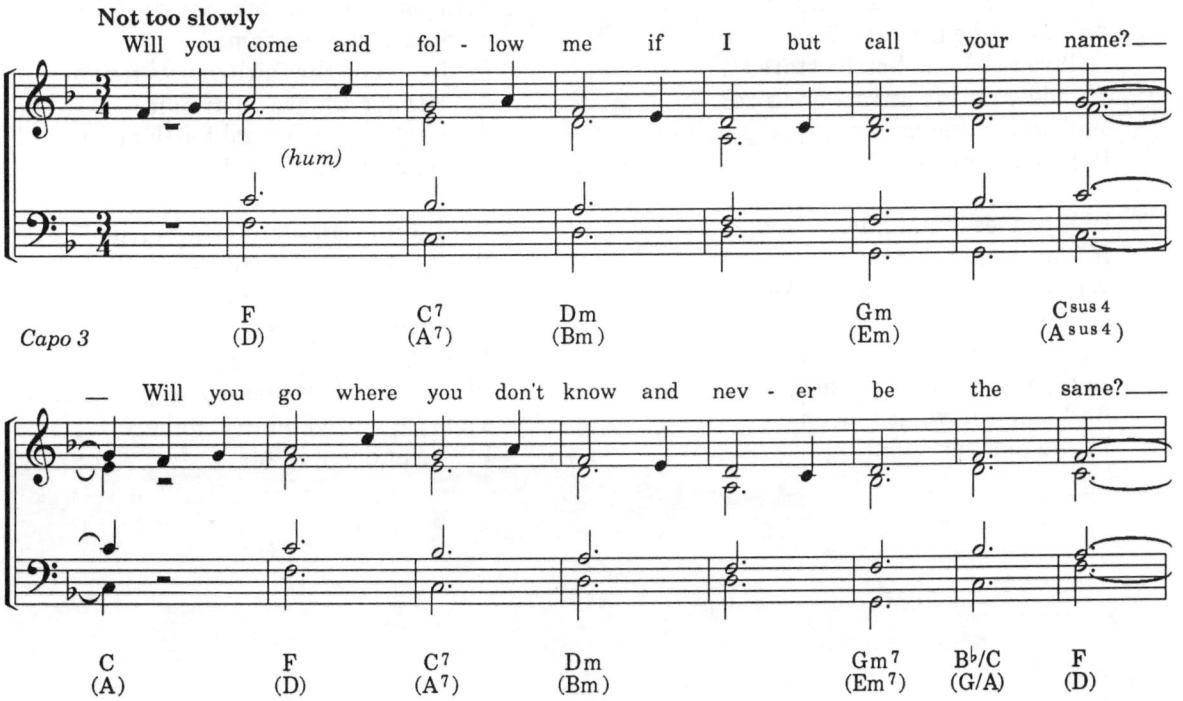

Not too slowly

Will you come and fol - low me if I but call your name?_____

(hum)

Capo 3   F   C⁷   Dm   Gm   C$^{sus 4}$
    (D)   (A⁷)   (Bm)   (Em)   (A$^{sus 4}$)

_____ Will you go where you don't know and nev - er be the same?_____

C   F   C⁷   Dm   Gm⁷   B♭/C   F
(A)   (D)   (A⁷)   (Bm)   (Em⁷)   (G/A)   (D)

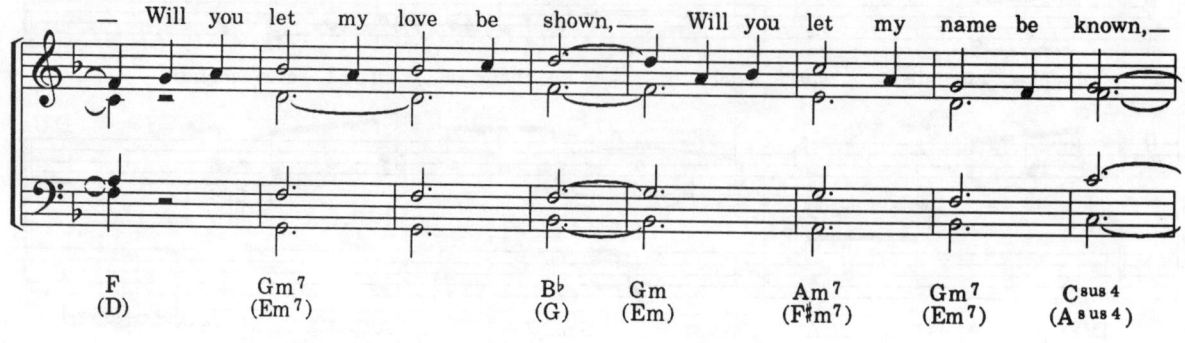

Will you let my love be shown,— Will you let my name be known,—

F (D)   Gm⁷ (Em⁷)   B♭ (G)   Gm (Em)   Am⁷ (F♯m⁷)   Gm⁷ (Em⁷)   Cˢᵘˢ ⁴ (Aˢᵘˢ ⁴)

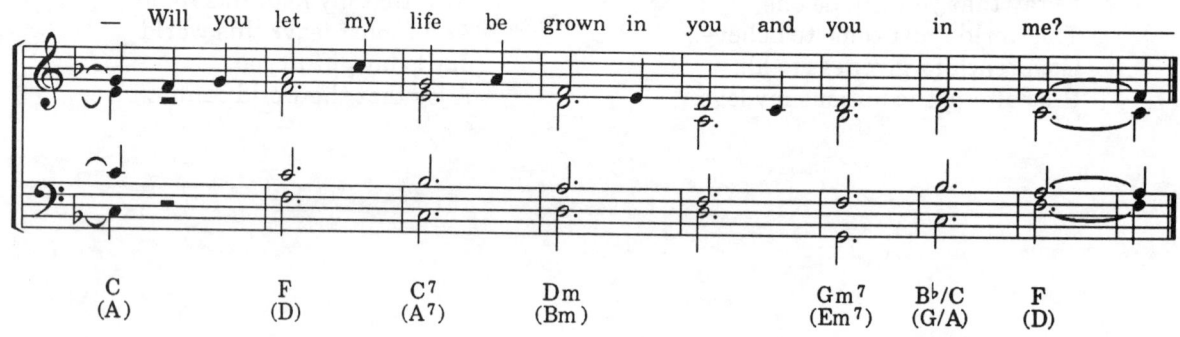

Will you let my life be grown in you and you in me?—

C (A)   F (D)   C⁷ (A⁷)   Dm (Bm)   Gm⁷ (Em⁷)   B♭/C (G/A)   F (D)

2 Will you leave yourself behind
   If I but call your name?
   Will you care for cruel and kind
   And never be the same?
   Will you risk the hostile stare
   Should your life attract or scare?
   Will you let me answer prayer
   In you and you in me?

3 Will you let the blinded see
   If I but call your name?
   Will you set the prisoners free
   And never be the same?
   Will you kiss the leper clean,
   And do such as this unseen,
   And admit to what I mean
   In you and you in me?

4 Will you love the "you" you hide
   If I but call your name?
   Will you quell the fear inside
   And never be the same?
   Will you use the faith you've found
   To reshape the world around,
   Through my sight and touch and sound
   In you and you in me?

5 Lord, your summons echoes true
   When you but call my name.
   Let me turn and follow you
   And never be the same.
   In your company I'll go
   Where your love and footsteps show.
   Thus I'll move and live and grow.
   In you and you in me.

235 King of All

Music and text adaptation: Feargal King

(based on Psalm 46(47))

Clap your hands, all peo-ple, shout to God with joy— for the Lord

Sing prai-ses to God,— sing prai-ses in a— psalm..

God———— has gone up———— with a shout, with the sound of a

Praise to the Lord of Hosts!

Note: This piece may be sung either as a round, or in the following way: sing A twice, then A + B twice then A+B+C (twice) then A+B+C+D twice, after which all voices go to the coda. The congregation should be encouraged to sing A while the choir adds on the other parts.

179

180

Instrumental parts

Intro +

A

(M.M. ♩ = 76-80)

24

B

(Sing praises . . .

C + **D**

(*Play this section 4 times*)

Coda

236 Beannacht leat a Mhuire
(Praise to God around us)

Bernard Sexton

182

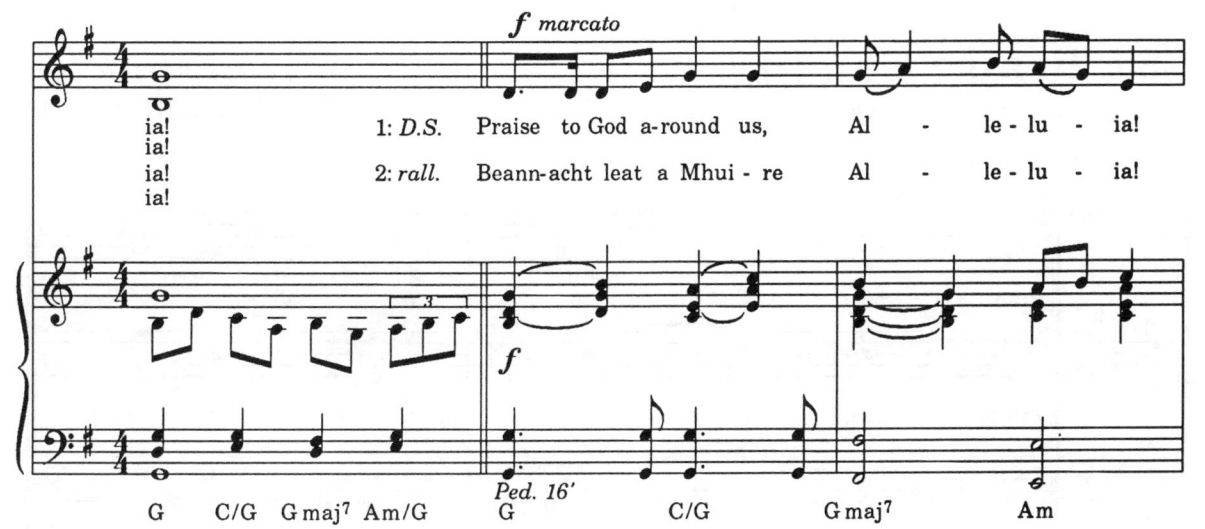

1: D.S. Praise to God a-round us, Al - le-lu - ia!
ia!
ia!
ia!

2: rall. Beann-acht leat a Mhui - re Al - le-lu - ia!

G   C/G Gmaj⁷ Am/G   G   C/G   Gmaj⁷   Am

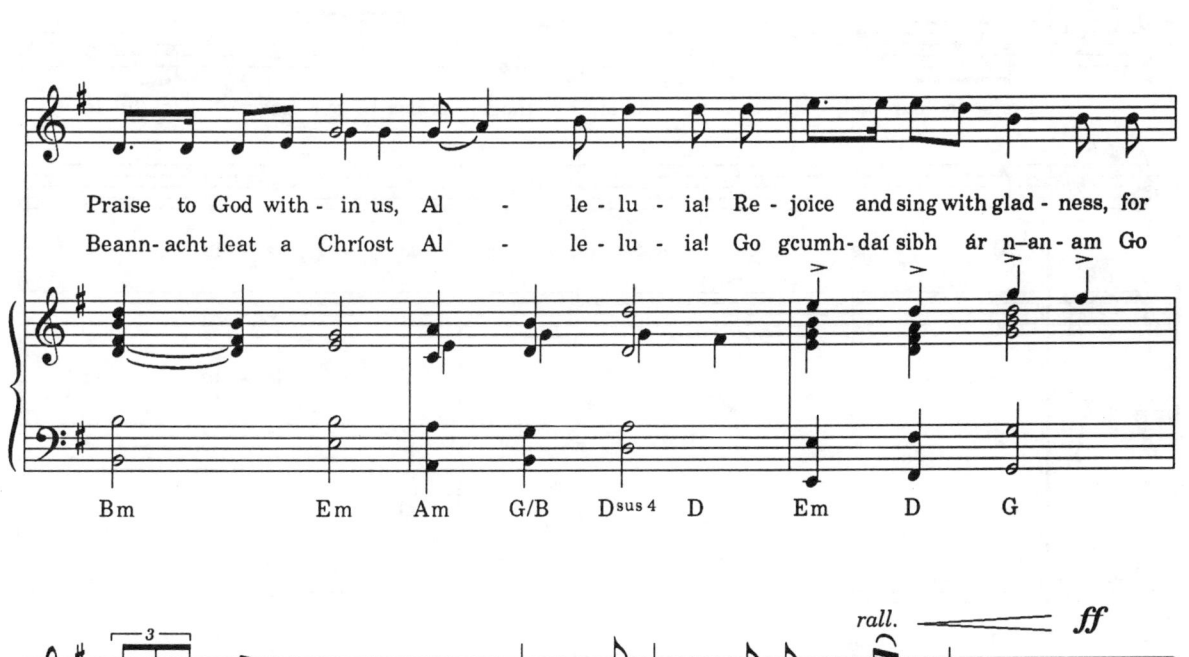

Praise   to God with - in us, Al - le - lu - ia! Re - joice and sing with glad - ness, for
Beann-acht leat a Chríost Al - le - lu - ia! Go gcumh-daí sibh ár n-an-am Go

Bm   Em   Am   G/B Dsus 4 D   Em   D   G

he— has saved his peo-ple. Al - le - lu - ia! Al - le - lu - ia!
dti - ge sin a - rís Al - le - lu - ia! Al - le - lu - ia!

Am   D   D⁷ G/B D/A   G   Em   Am   D   G

237 Praise Canon

for voices, with optional instrumental doubling

Words: Patrick Lee
Music : Alan Smith

Steady and strong!

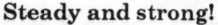

1. Praise our God, One un - di - vi - ded.

2. Praise to our God, the Fa-ther cre - a - tor; praise to our God. Al - le - lu - ia.

3. Praise to our God, his Son, the re - deem - er; praise to our God. Al - le - lu - ia.

4. Praise to our God, the Spi - rit who streng - thens; praise to our God. Al - le - lu - ia.

5. Al - le - lu - ia, al - le - lu - ia.

6. Al - le - lu - ia, al - le - lu - ia.

7. Al - le - lu - ia, al - le - lu - ia.

8. Al - le - lu - ia, al - le - lu - ia.

Em   Bm   Am/C   Em   Am   G/B Am/C   Em

Suggestions for performance

Don't perform this too quickly. 90 b.p.m. or less would be about right.

Parts 1–5 are intended for the assembly and parts 6–7 for the choir, but you can be flexible about this.

Use melody and rhythm instruments freely to double or even replace the voices. Encourage improvisation.

Aim for a robust "medieval" sound. Starting with part 1, perform each part twice before bringing in the next one.

238 Were we with you, Jesus?

Text: Paul Gardner
Music: Ray d'Inverno

1 Were we with you, Je-sus, when they took you to the court? Could you hear us, Je-sus, when you listen-ed for su-pport? su-ffered for our sake?

2 Did we speak up, Jesus,
   When your teaching was denounced?
   Did we protest, Jesus,
   When the sentence was pronounced?

3 Were we silent, Jesus,
   When they asked us where we stood?
   Were we faithful, Jesus,
   When they nailed you to the wood?

4 Did we realize, Jesus,
   When the earth began to shake,
   That here was God's son Jesus
   Who had suffered for our sake?

Alternative (4th verse)

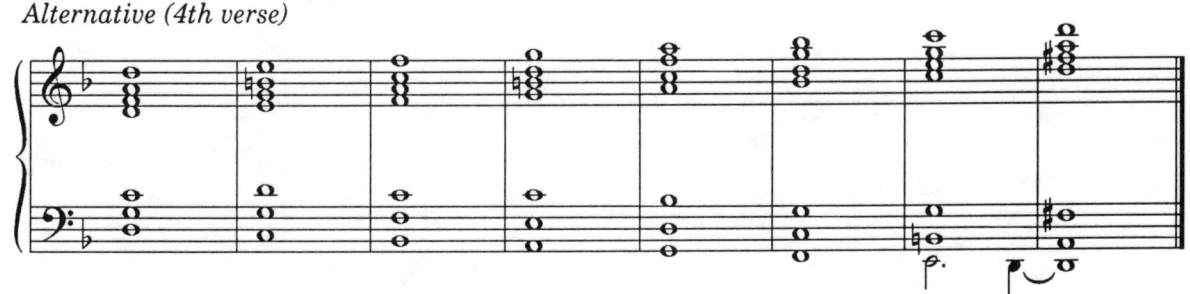

239 Passion Sunday: Entrance Song

Alan Rees

The initial Hosannas are sung by the choir, repeated by All. The choir then continues, dividing into two parts for "Blessed is he ...". The final line is repeated by everyone after the choir.

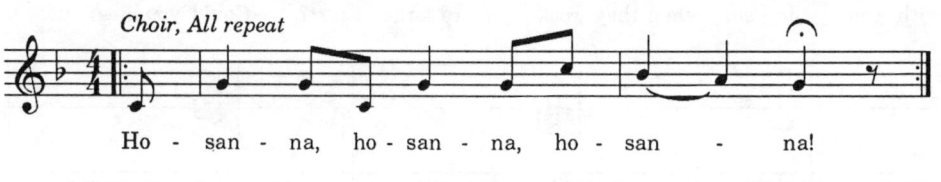

Ho - san - na, ho - san - na, ho - san - na!

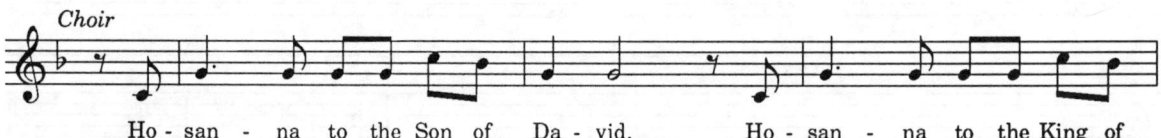

Ho - san - na to the Son of Da - vid. Ho - san - na to the King of

Is - ra - el!

Bless - ed is he who comes in the name of the Lord.

Ho - san - na, ho - san - na in the high - est!

240 Passion Sunday:
Music for the Commemoration
of the Lord's Entry into Jerusalem

Chris McCurry

240A Entrance Antiphon (Round)

If there is a choir to sustain the round in four parts, the congregation could sing just the first line repeatedly, where it is not possible for them to learn it all.

Note: Either or both of the verses may be sung over the round by a strong solo voice or a group of voices, with or without microphone. Normally, however, it will not be desirable to extend this part of the liturgy for too long. Chords in brackets: Capo 3.

240B Procession: (a) Outside

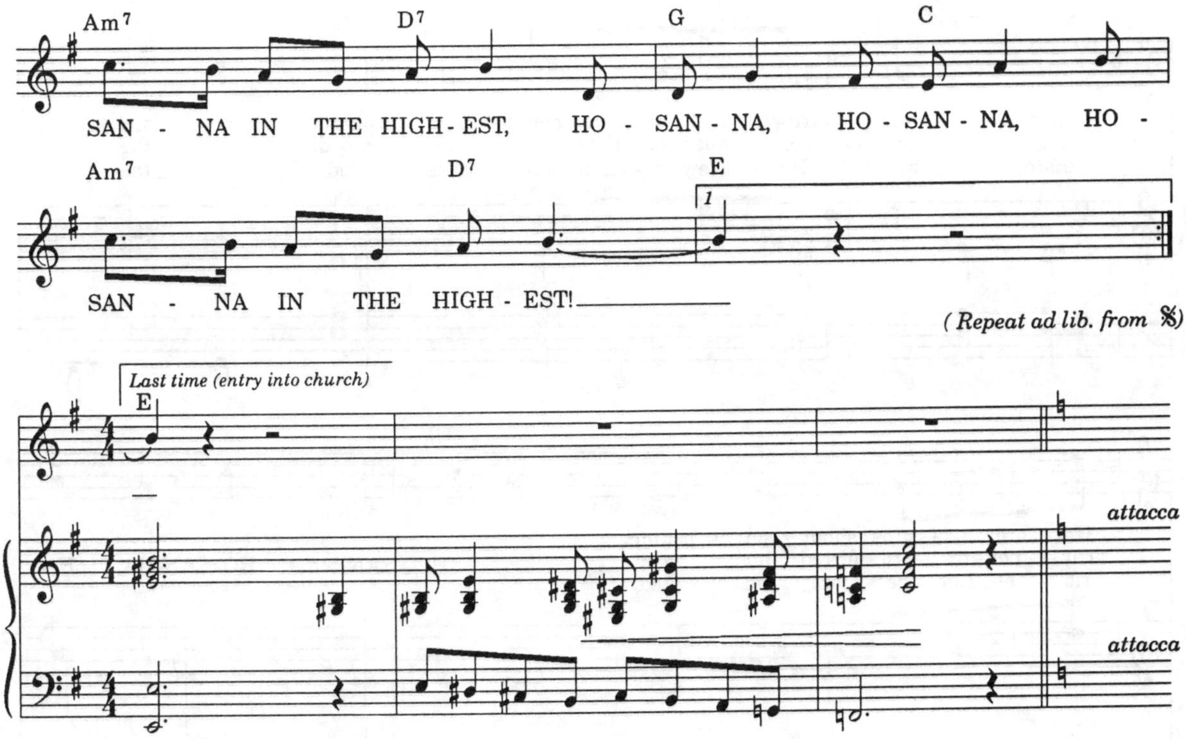
Am7 D7 G C
SAN - NA IN THE HIGH - EST, HO - SAN - NA, HO - SAN - NA, HO -
Am7 D7 E
1
SAN - NA IN THE HIGH - EST!
(Repeat ad lib. from 𝄋)
Last time (entry into church)
E
attacca
attacca

(b) Entering church

Words: "Ingrediente Domino" by Michael Hodgetts

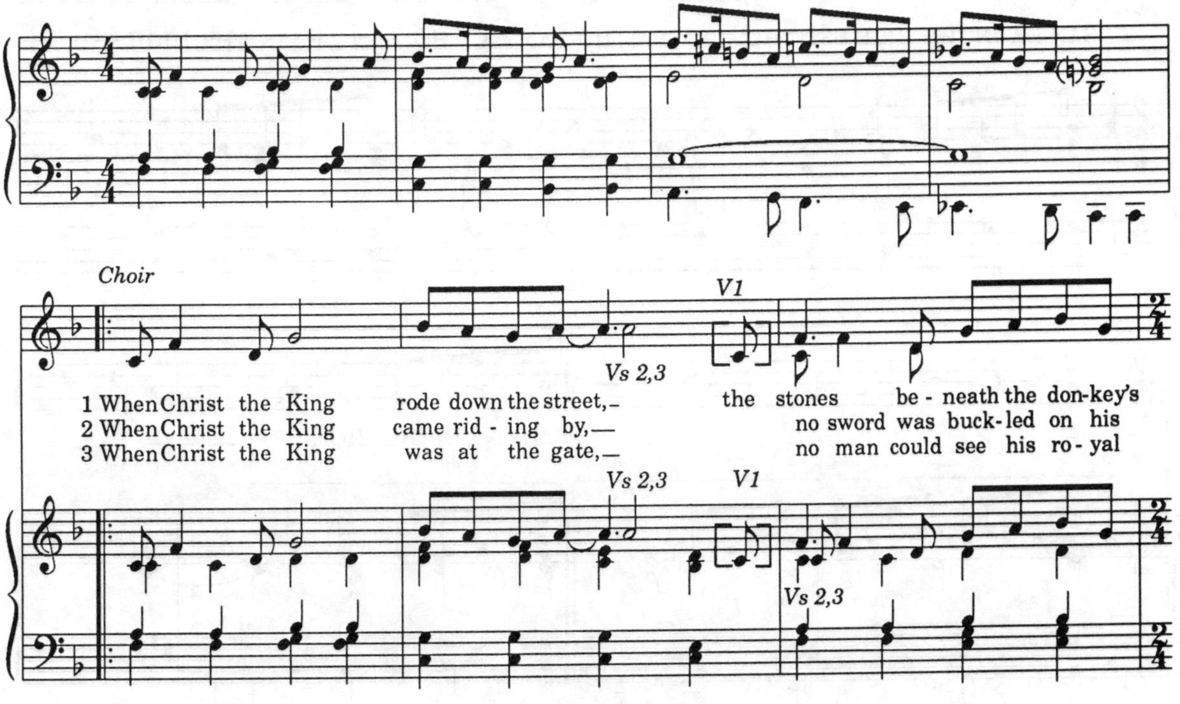
Choir
V1
Vs 2,3
1 When Christ the King rode down the street, – the stones be - neath the don-key's
2 When Christ the King came rid - ing by, — no sword was buck-led on his
3 When Christ the King was at the gate, – no man could see his ro - yal
Vs 2,3
V1
Vs 2,3

feet were strewn with o-live-boughs and palms, and
thigh. A con-quer-or they un-der-stood: and the
state; but He-brew ur-chins pro-phes-ied the

All.

He-brew ur-chins shout-ed psalms.
car-pen-ter pre-ferred his wood.
ris-en Life be-fore he died.

HO-SAN-NA, HO-SAN-NA, HO-

SAN-NA IN THE HIGH-EST! HO-SAN-NA, HO-SAN-NA, HO-SAN-NA IN THE HIGH-EST!

1,2

SAN-NA IN THE HIGH-EST!

3

241 Passion Sunday: Responsorial Psalm 21(22)

Alan Smith

Note: Organists may find it helpful to repeat the chord at the beginning of the bar where each verse starts, to clarify the rhythm for the singer(s).

sem - bled.   You who fear the Lord give him praise;   all   sons of   Ja - cob,

give him glo - ry.   Re - vere him,   Is - rael's sons.   My

God,   my God,   why have you   for - sa - ken   me?

242 Passion Sunday and Good Friday: *harm. J S Bach*
Gospel Acclamation

1 Christ was hum - bler yet,_____ e - ven to ac -
2 But God raised him high,_____ and gave him the

cep - ting death, death_____ on a cross.
name_____ ting which is a - bove all names.

243 Holy Thursday: *Music: Sue Furlong*
Responsorial Psalm 115(116):
The blessing cup

Adagio (♩=66)

Dm   Dm⁷   G/B   Gm/B♭   Dm   Aˢᵘˢ⁴   A   Aˢᵘˢ⁴

Response

The blessing cup— that we bless_____ is com- mun-ion with the blood of

Ah

A⁷   Dm   Dm⁷   G/B   Gm/B♭

194

Christ. The bless-ing cup— that we bless— is com-

Dm   Dm   Dm⁷   E♭

mun - ion with the blood of Christ.

Aˢᵘˢ ⁴   A   Dm

Verses

1 How can I re-pay the Lord for his good-ness to me? The

Dm   Dm⁷   Gm/B♭   Dm

cup of sal-va-tion I will raise; I will call on the Lord's name.

Refrain

Dm   Dm⁷   E♭   Aˢᵘˢ ⁴   A⁷   Dm

195

2 O pre-cious in the eyes of the Lord is the death of his faith-ful. Your ser-vant, Lord, your ser-vant am I; you have loos-ened my bonds. 3 A thanks-giv-ing sac-ri-fice I make; I will call on the Lord's name. My vows— to the Lord I will ful-fil be-fore all his peo-ple.

Refrain

Refrain

244 Faith, Hope and Love
Christopher Walker

(Mandatum)
Refrain based on 1 Cor 13

Intro: *Gently* (♩ = 92)

Refrain

Descant or Solo Instr.

Soprano (Melody) Alto

Tenor Bass

Faith, Hope and Love, let

Faith,— Hope and Love,— let

p

p

(p)

these re-main a-mong you. Faith,____ Hope and

these re-main a-mong you.____ Faith,____ Hope and

Love. The great-est of these is Love.____ Love.____

Love.____ The great-est of these is Love. Love.

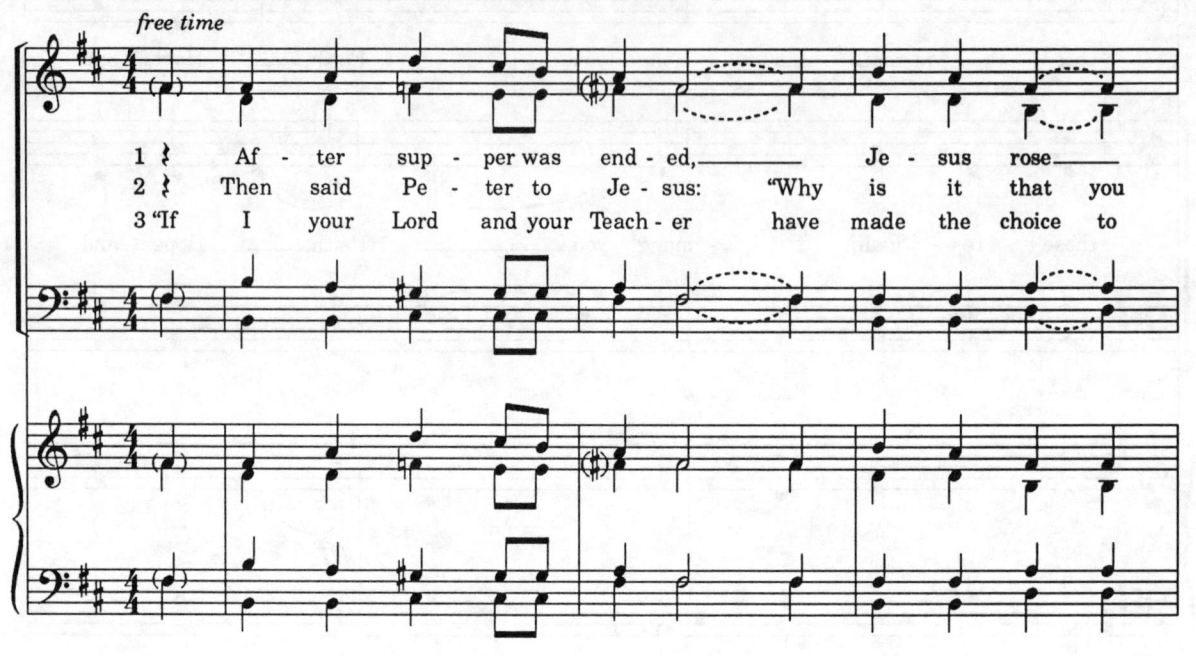

1 After supper was ended,___ Je-sus rose___
2 Then said Pe-ter to Je-sus: "Why is it that you
3 "If I your Lord and your Teach-er have made the choice to

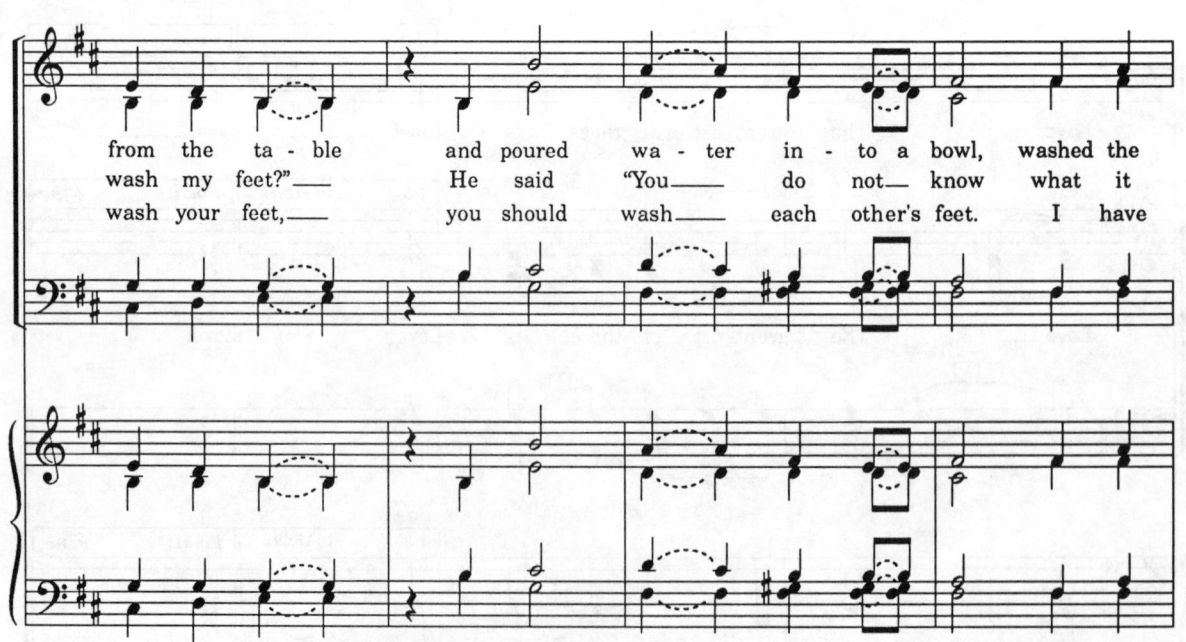

from the ta-ble and poured wa-ter in-to a bowl, washed the
wash my feet?"___ He said "You___ do not___ know what it
wash your feet,___ you should wash___ each other's feet. I have

* Alternative verses from Ubi Caritas can be found on page 200.

198

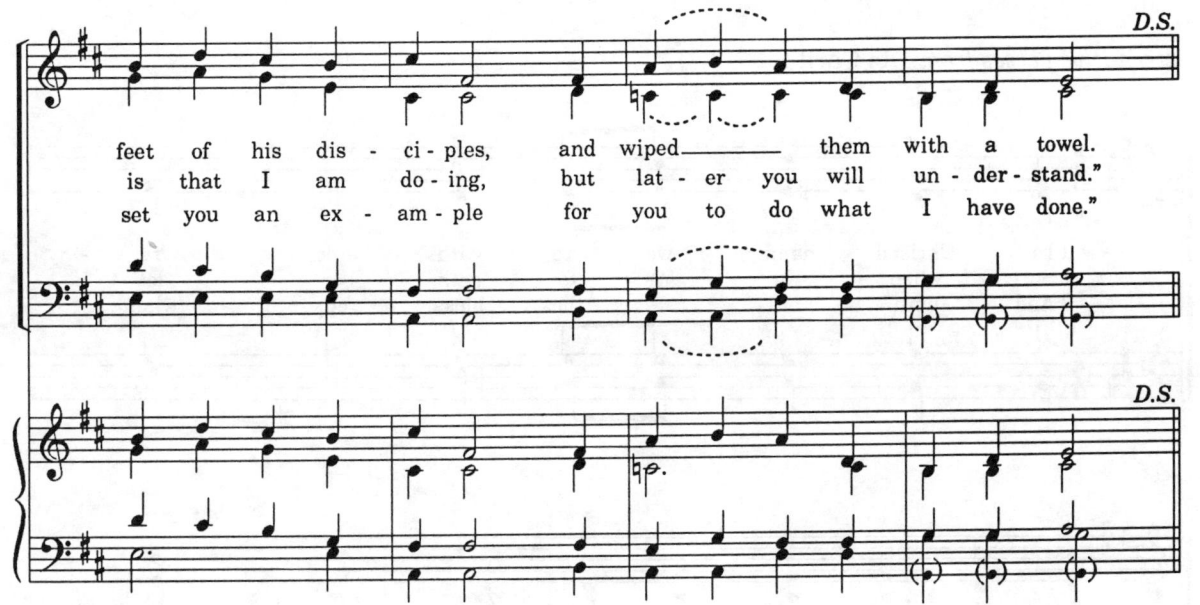

feet of his dis - ci - ples, and wiped＿＿＿ them with a towel.
is that I am do - ing, but lat - er you will un - der - stand."
set you an ex - am - ple for you to do what I have done."

Alternative verses from Ubi Caritas

1 In Christ's name we are gath - ered; re -
2 So when we are to - geth - er let
3 And with all of the bless - ed, when

joice in Christ, be glad in him. For our
us be one in heart and mind, re - move
earth is gone and time is still, with pure

God is ev - er liv - ing. Let us fear and love God
bit - ter - ness and strife;_____ let there be an end to
love in you our God,_____ may we see your face in

D.S.

al - ways and love each oth - er from our hearts.
quar - rels and in our midst be Christ our God.
glo - ry and praise you with un - end - ing joy.

245 Good Friday: Responsorial Psalm

Plainchant, arr. G B S

Response

Fa - ther, in - to your hands I com-mend my—— spi - rit.

Geoffrey Boulton Smith

Psalm-Tone

Psalm 30(31)

1 In you, O Lord, | I take | refuge.
 Let me never be | put to | shame.
 In your justice set me free. Into your hands I com | mend my | spirit.
 It is you who will re | deem me, | Lord. *R.*

2 In the face of | all my | foes
 I am | a re | proach,
 an object of scorn | to my | neighbours
 and of fear | to my | friends. *R.*

3 Those who see me | in the | street
 run far a | way from | me.
 I am like a dead man, forgotten | in men's | hearts,
 like a thing | thrown a | way. *R.*

4 But as for me, I | trust in · you, | Lord,
 I say: "You | are my | God."
 My life is in your | hands, de | liver me͡
 from the hands of | those who | hate me. *R.*

5 Let your face shine | on your | servant,
 Save me | in your | love.
 Be strong, let your | heart take | courage,
 all who hope | in the | Lord. *R.*

246 Good Friday:
Veneration of the Cross: the Invitation

Geoffrey Boulton Smith

This is repeated three times, each time beginning a tone higher, the note on which the people finish.

247 Good Friday:
Processional Song of the Cross

Text: Harold Winstone

Music: Paul Inwood

This song may be used in the procession of the Cross. It is sung continuously and not three times as with This is the wood of the cross. It is similar to the former, however, in having parts for the priest to sing, in dialogue with cantor and All.

All repeat refrain from "Come, come, let us adore". Then the whole of the refrain is repeated, i.e. first the priest then All sing the whole refrain. V2 follows:

Dear-est wood and dear-est iron, dear-est weight is hung there-on.

D.S. 𝄋

Ne - ver was a tree so fair, none in E - den was thy peer.

*The procedure following verse 1 is repeated. All repeat refrain from "Come, come, let us adore".
Then the whole of the refrain is repeated, i.e. first the priest then All sing the whole refrain, to
conclude the song.*

248 Good Friday:

Paul Inwood

O my people: Reproaches for Good Friday

for Joan Grace and the musicians and people of Wadhurst

(♩ = 54)

Choir (unison), All repeat

O MY PEO - PLE, WHAT HAVE I DONE TO YOU?

Em   Em/D   C   Em⁷/B

HOW HAVE I HURT YOU? ANS - WER ME. I

Am⁷   Em⁷   Am⁶   B⁷

(to page 208)

Repeat
"Holy is God"
(page 205)

Cantor / Choir

2 more could I have done for you? I plant-ed you as my

[O MY PEO - PLE, WHAT HAVE I DONE TO YOU?

All may sing the refrain softly

Em   Em/D   C   Em⁷/B

fair - est vine,_____ but you yield - ed on - ly bit - ter - ness:

HOW HAVE I HURT_ YOU? AN - SWER ME.

Am⁷   Em⁷   Am⁶   B⁷

when I was thirst - y you gave me vi - ne - gar to

O MY PEO - PLE, WHAT HAVE I DONE TO YOU?

Em   Em/D   C   Em⁷/B

drink, and you pierced your Sa-viour with a lance.

HOW HAVE I HURT_ YOU? AN - SWER ME.]

Repeat "Holy is God" (page 205); then continue on page 208.

Am⁷   Em⁷   Am⁶   B⁷

207

Vocal (or instrumental) descant

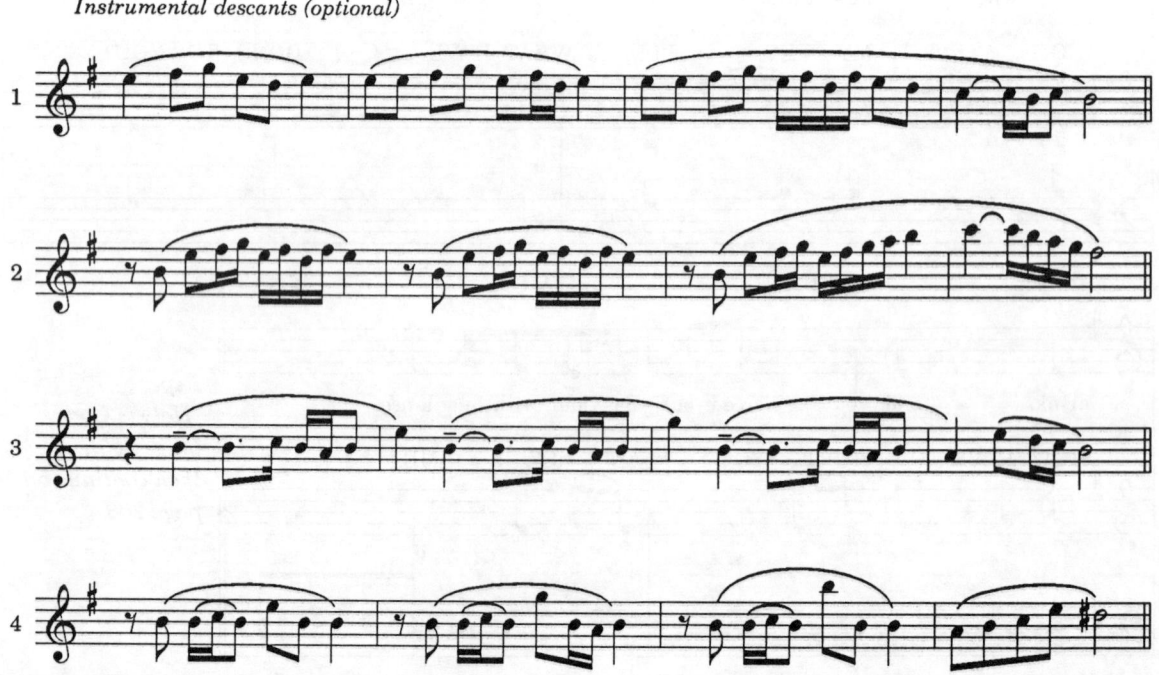

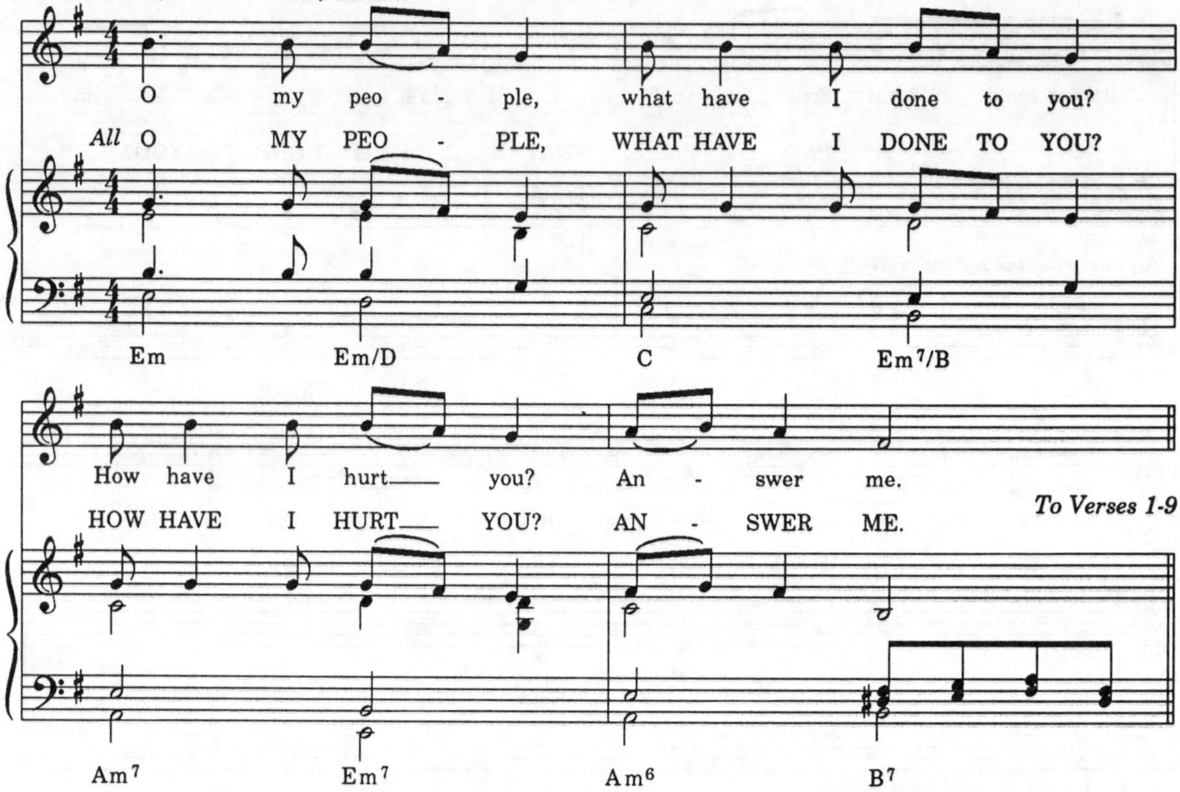

Instrumental descants (optional)

1. For your sake I scourged your cap-tors and their first-born sons, but

2. I led you to free-dom, drowned your cap-tors in the sea, but you

3. I o-pened the sea be-fore you, but you

4. I led you on your way in a pil-lar of cloud, but

5. I bore you up with man-na in the de-sert, but you

6. I gave you sa-ving wa-ter from the rock, but you

7. For you I struck down the kings of Ca-na-an, but

E   Am(7)   Dm   G(7)

1. you brought your scour-ges down on me.

Repeat "O MY PEOPLE"
page 208

2. hand-ed me o-ver to your priests.

Repeat "O MY PEOPLE"
page 208

3. o-pened my side with a spear.

Repeat "O MY PEOPLE"
page 208

4. you led me to Pi-late's court.

Repeat "O MY PEOPLE"
page 208

5. struck me down and scourged me.

Repeat "O MY PEOPLE"
page 208

6. gave me gall and vi-ne-gar to drink.

Repeat "O MY PEOPLE"
page 208

7. you struck my head with a reed.

Repeat "O MY PEOPLE"
page 208

C   Am   B⁷ˢᵘˢ   B

8. I gave you a roy-al scep-tre, but

9. I raised you to the height of ma-jest-y, but

E   Am⁽⁷⁾   D   G(maj⁷)

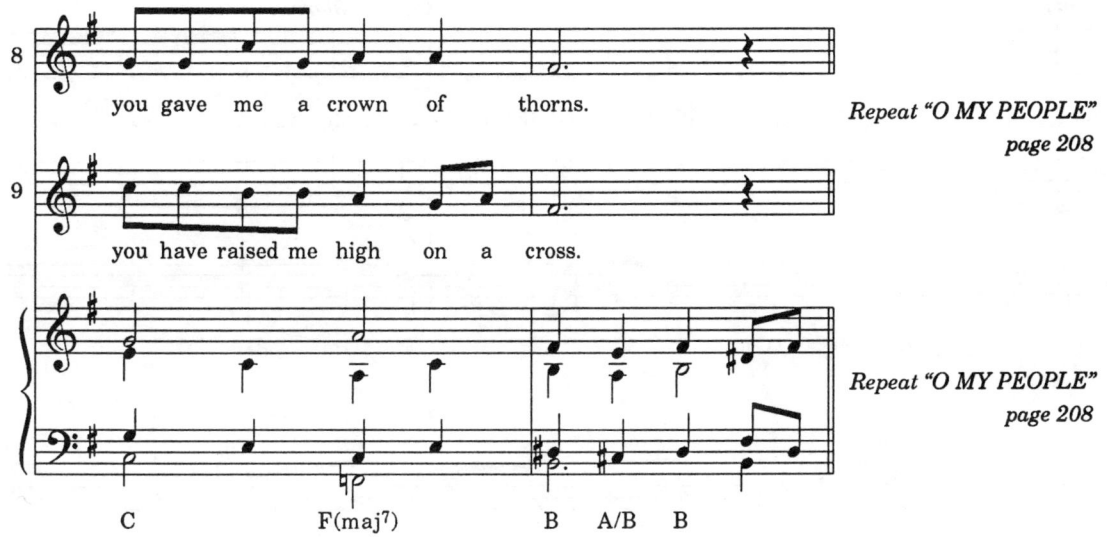

you gave me a crown of thorns.

Repeat "O MY PEOPLE"
page 208

you have raised me high on a cross.

Repeat "O MY PEOPLE"
page 208

C   F(maj⁷)   B   A/B   B

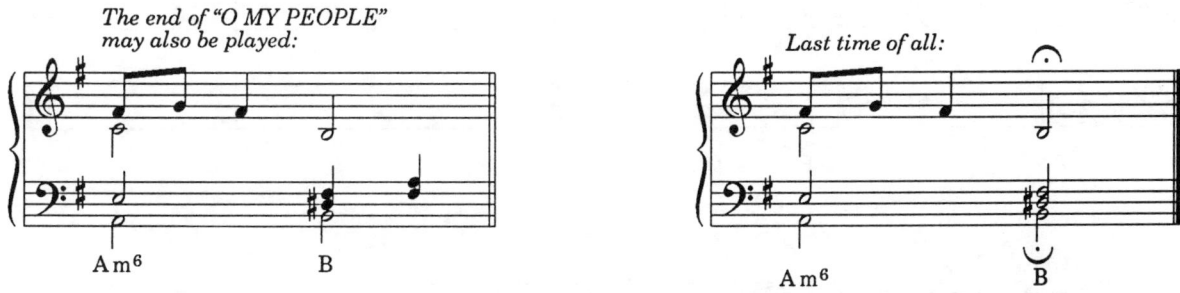

The end of "O MY PEOPLE"
may also be played:

Am⁶   B

Last time of all:

Am⁶   B

The music of this piece is continuous; there should be no breaks between verses and refrains.

249 Easter Vigil: Exsultet (short form)

Geoffrey Boulton Smith

Tempo giusto (♩= c. 88)

Cantor / Choir

All

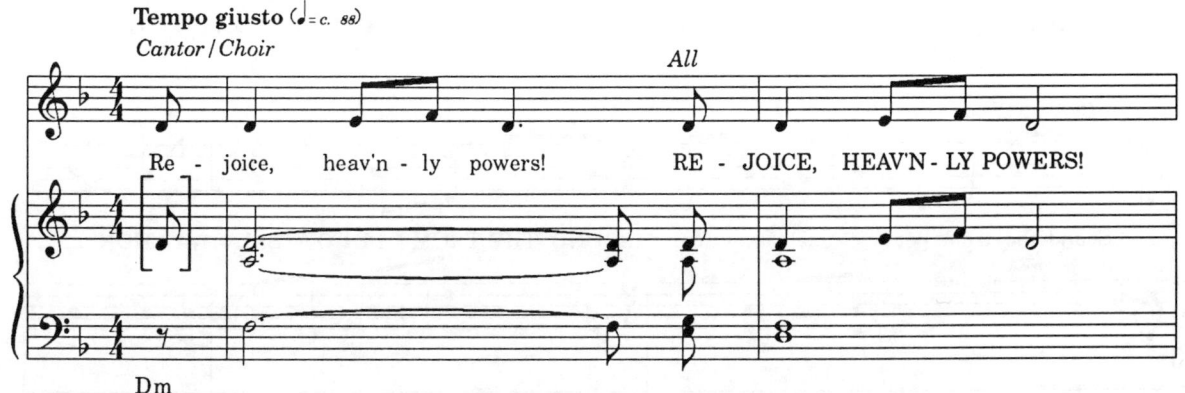

Re - joice,   heav'n - ly   powers!   RE - JOICE,   HEAV'N - LY POWERS!

Dm

If guitars are used to accompany this Exsultet they may strum in the refrains, but should accompany the solo Cantors with guitar chords only where they are marked, in the manner of lute accompaniment to recitative.

JOICE, HEAV'-LY POWERS! SING, CHOIRS OF AN-GELS! EX-

Dm   Gm   C

Tempo comodo
Cantor

ULT, ALL CRE-A-TION A-ROUND GOD'S THRONE! *Lift up your hearts.

F Gm Dm C Am Dm C

All   *Cantor*

WE LIFT THEM UP TO THE LORD. Let us give thanks to the Lord our God.

Dm Gm C Dm Dm Gm

All

IT IS RIGHT TO GIVE HIM THANKS AND PRAISE.

B♭   Gm⁷   C

214

and led them dry - shod through the sea. RE -

JOICE, HEAVN'-LY POWERS! SING, CHOIRS OF AN- GELS! EX -

ULT, ALL CRE - A - TION A - ROUND GOD'S THRONE!

Tempo comodo
Cantor I

This is the night when Christ- ians ev - ery - where,—

washed clean of sin and freed from all de - file - ment,

are re - stored to grace and grow to - ge - ther in ho - li - ness.

Cantor II

This is the night when Je - sus Christ broke the chains of death

Tempo I
All

and rose tri - umphant from the grave. JE - SUS CHRIST, OUR KING, IS RI - SEN!

SOUND THE TRUM - PET OF SAL - VA - TION!_____

Dm   Gm   A

Tempo comodo
Cantor II

Fa - ther, how wond - er - ful your care for us! How bound - less your mer - ci - ful love!

G   D   Dm   G   Em   D

Cantor I

To ransom a slave you gave a - way your Son. O hap-py fault, O nec - ess - a - ry sin of A - dam,

G   D   Em   Bm   Em   Em   Bm

Tempo I
All

which gained for us so great a Re - deem - er! RE - JOICE, HEAVN'LY POWERS!

Em   Am⁷   Bm   Em

219

SING, CHOIRS OF AN-GELS! EX - ULT, ALL CRE - A - TION AROUND GOD'S

Am   D   G   Am   Em   D

Tempo comodo
Cantor I

THRONE! The power of this ho - ly night dis - pels all e - vil, wa-shes guilt a - way,

Bm   Em   Am   D   D   G

re - stores lost in - no - cence,_____ brings mourn - ers joy.

Em   A   Em   Bm

Cantor II

Night tru - ly bless - ed when heav - en is wed - ded to earth

G   D   G   D

and man is re-con-ciled with God! JE - SUS CHRIST, OUR KING, IS RI - SEN!

SOUND THE TRUM - PET OF SAL - VA - TION!

Therefore, heavn'ly Fa-ther, in the joy of this night, re-ceive our evening sac-ri-fice of praise,

your Church's so - lemn off - er - ing. Ac - cept this Eas - ter can - dle.

May it al - ways dis - pel the dark - ness of this night!

G   G   D

Cantors I and II

May the Morn - ing Star which ne - ver sets find this flame still burn - ing:

Em   Bm   C   D   G   D

Christ, that Morning Star, who came back from the dead, and shed his peaceful light on all mankind,

Em   Bm Em Am⁷   Bm   Am⁷   D

Tempo I
All

your Son, who lives and reigns for e - ver and e - ver. RE -

C   C   Am⁷   Bm

222

JOICE, HEAV'NLY POWERS! SING, CHOIRS OF AN-GELS! EX -

Em   Am   D

ULT, ALL CRE - A - TION A-ROUND GOD'S THRONE!

G   Am   Em   D   Bm

JE - SUS CHRIST, OUR KING, IS RI - SEN! SOUND THE TRUM-PET OF SAL -

Em   D   Em   Am   Em   Am

VA - TION!_____ A - MEN, A - MEN.

B   D   Em   Bm⁷   E

*If the dialogue of page 214, bars 5–8 is omitted,
the solo for Cantor I on page 215 should begin as follows:

It is tru - ly right. . . .

etc.

223

250 Easter Vigil:
The first Reading from Genesis (1:1–22)

Christopher Walker

The recurring phrase at the end of each day of creation may be treated as a sung antiphon thus:

251 Easter Vigil:
Responsorial Psalms

Chris McCurry

251A After 1st Reading (Psalm 103(104))

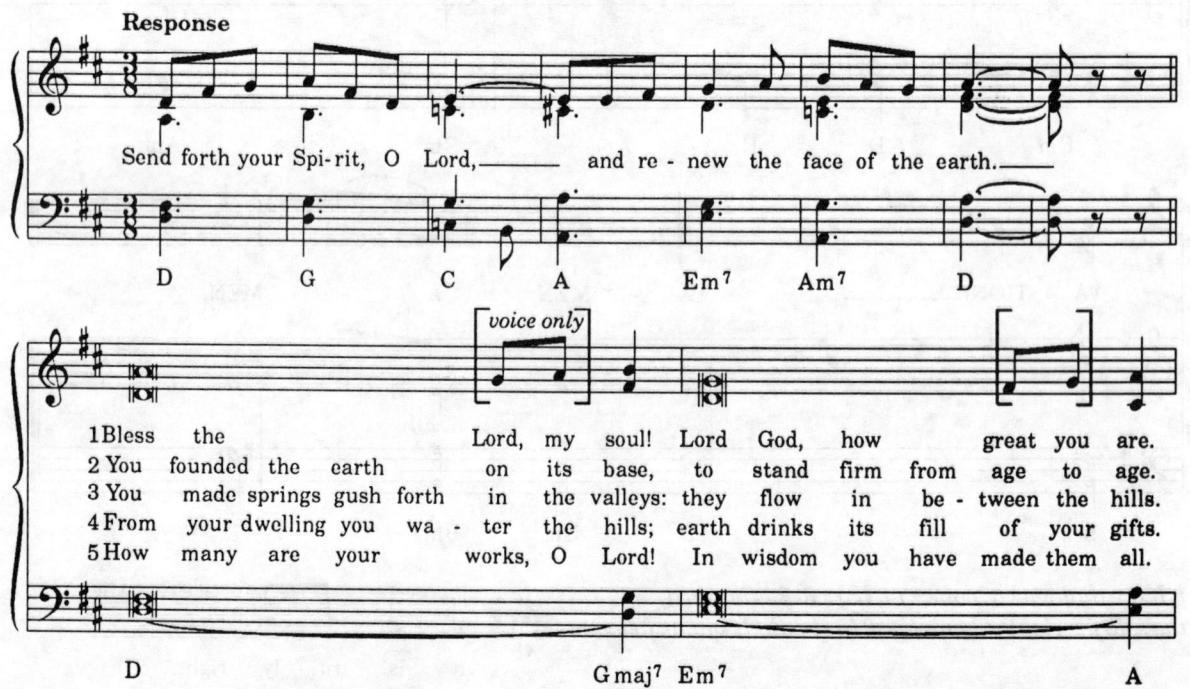

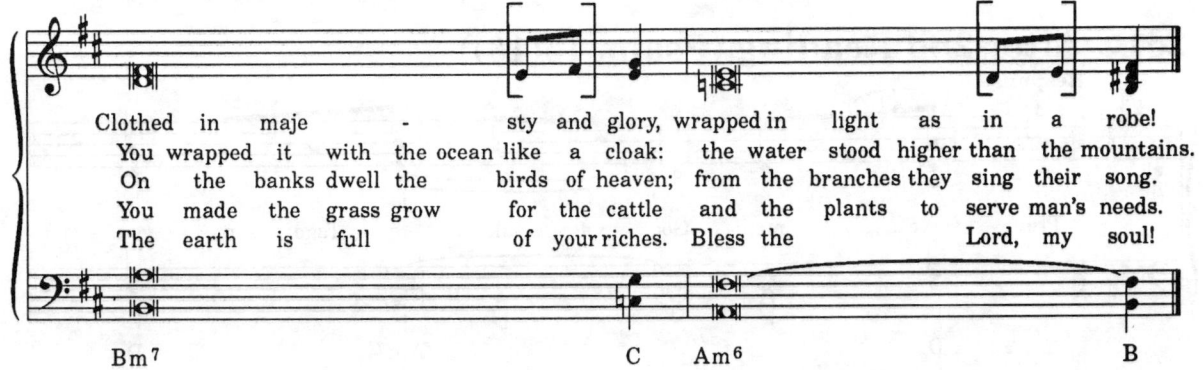

Clothed in maje - sty and glory, wrapped in light as in a robe!
You wrapped it with the ocean like a cloak: the water stood higher than the mountains.
On the banks dwell the birds of heaven; from the branches they sing their song.
You made the grass grow for the cattle and the plants to serve man's needs.
The earth is full of your riches. Bless the Lord, my soul!

Bm⁷   C   Am⁶   B

251B Alternative Psalm after 1st Reading (Psalm 32(33))

Response

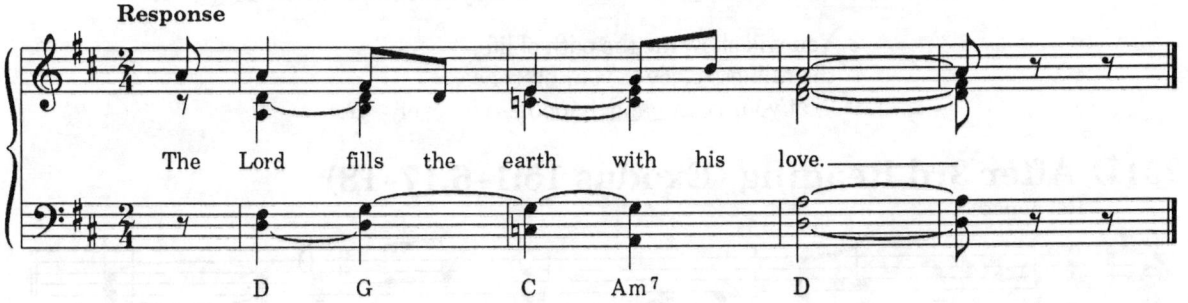

The Lord fills the earth with his love.

D   G   C   Am⁷   D

1 The word of the Lórd is <u>faith</u>ful
and all his works tó be <u>trust</u>ed.
The Lord loves justíce and <u>right</u>
and fills the earth wíth his <u>love</u>.   ℟.

2 By his word the heavéns were <u>made</u>,
by the breath of his mouth áll the <u>stars</u>.
He collects the waves óf the <u>ocean</u>;
he stores up the depths óf the <u>sea</u>.   ℟.

3 They are happy, whose God ís the <u>Lord</u>,
the people he has chosen ás his <u>own</u>.
From the heavens the Lórd looks <u>forth</u>,
he sees all the childrén of <u>men</u>.   ℟.

4 Our soul is waiting fór the <u>Lord</u>.
The Lord is our help ánd our <u>shield</u>.
May your love be upon ús, O <u>Lord</u>,
as we place all our hópe in <u>you</u>.   ℟.

Note: For all the psalms 268A to 268I use the same psalm tone, given in full here for Psalm 103(104) and again for Exodus 15.

251C After 2nd Reading (Psalm 15(16))

Response

Pre- serve___ me, God, I take re- fuge in you.

D   C   Am⁷   D

1 O Lord, it is you who are my portión and cup;
it is you yourself who áre my prize.
I keep the Lord ever ín my sight:
since he is at my right hand, I sháll stand firm. ℟.

2 And so my heart rejoices, my sóul is glad;
even my body shall rést in safety.
For you will not leave my soul amóng the dead,
nor let your beloved knów decay. ℟.

3 You will show me the páth of life,
the fullness of joy ín your presence,
(†) at yóur right hand happinéss for ever. ℟.

251D After 3rd Reading (Exodus 15:1–6,17–18)

Response

I will sing to the Lord, glo- rious his tri- umph!___

D   G   C   Am⁷   D

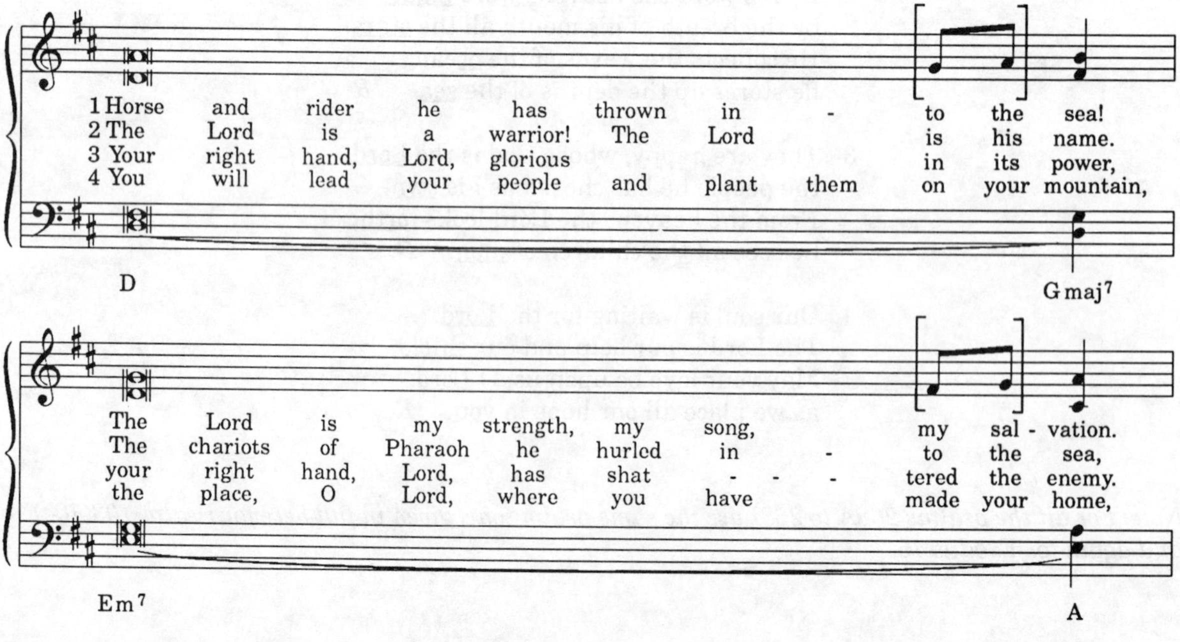

1 Horse   and   rider   he   has   thrown   in -   to   the   sea!
2 The   Lord   is   a   warrior! The   Lord   is   his   name.
3 Your   right   hand,   Lord,   glorious   in   its   power,
4 You   will   lead   your   people   and   plant   them   on   your   mountain,

D   G maj⁷

The   Lord   is   my   strength,   my   song,   my   sal -   vation.
The   chariots   of   Pharaoh   he   hurled   in -   to   the   sea,
your   right   hand,   Lord,   has   shat - -   tered   the   enemy.
the   place,   O   Lord,   where   you   have   made   your   home,

Em⁷   A

226

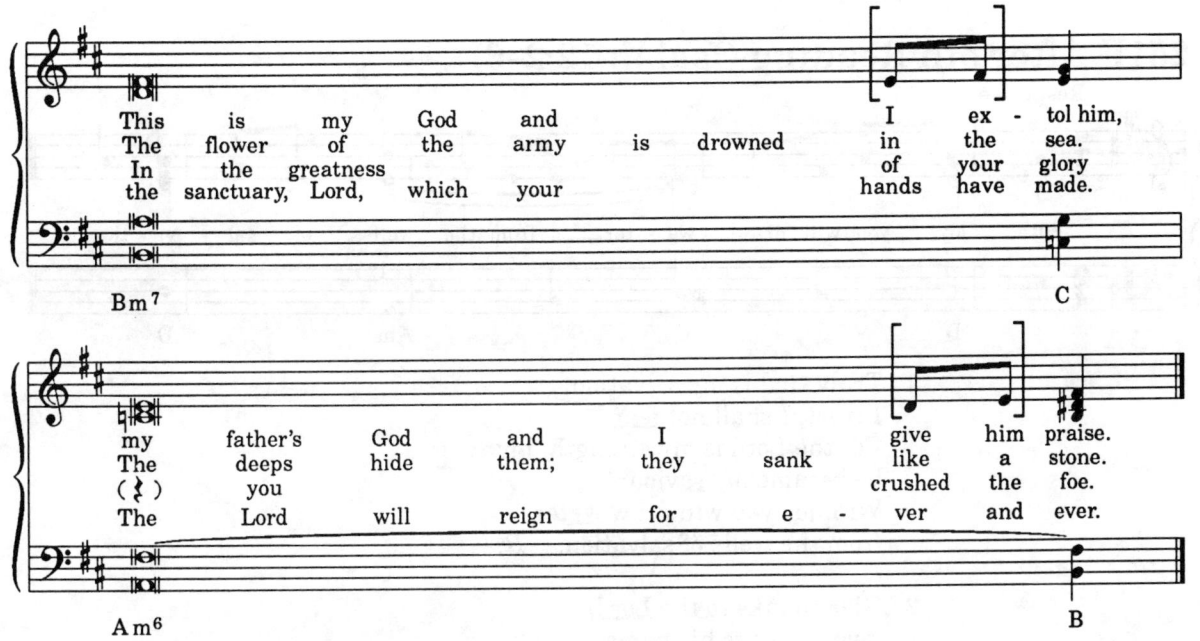

This is my God and I ex - tol him,
The flower of the army is drowned in the sea.
In the greatness of your glory
the sanctuary, Lord, which your hands have made.

Bm⁷   C

my father's God and I give him praise.
The deeps hide them; they sank like a stone.
(𝄽) you crushed the foe.
The Lord will reign for e - ver and ever.

Am⁶   B

251E After 4th Reading (Psalm 29(30))

Response

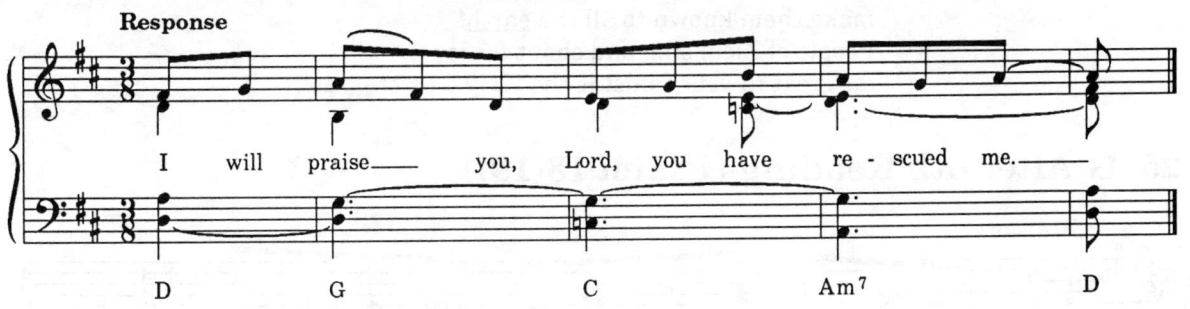

I will praise you, Lord, you have re - scued me.

D   G   C   Am⁷   D

1 I will praise you, Lord, yóu have <u>res</u>cued me
and have not let my enemies rejoice óver <u>me</u>.
O Lord, you have raised my soul fróm the <u>dead</u>,
restored me to life from those who sink intó the <u>grave</u>.   ℞.

2 Sing psalms to the Lord, yóu who <u>love</u> him,
give thanks to his hóly <u>name</u>.
His anger lasts but a moment; his favóur through <u>life</u>.
At night there are tears, but joy cómes with <u>dawn</u>.   ℞.

3 The Lord listened ánd had <u>pity</u>.
The Lord came tó my <u>help</u>.
For me you have changed my mourning intó <u>dancing</u>,
O Lord my God, I will thank yóu for <u>ever</u>.   ℞.

251F After 5th Reading (Isaiah 12:2–6)

Response

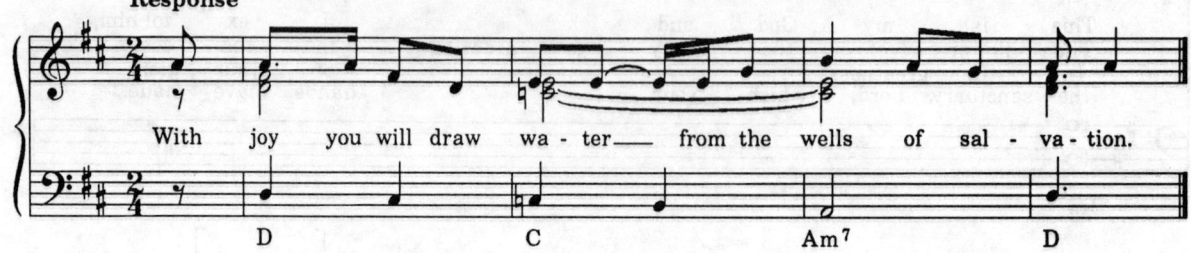

With joy you will draw wa-ter— from the wells of sal - va - tion.

1 Truly God is my salvation,
   I trust, I sháll not <u>fear</u>.
   For the Lord is my strength, my song,
   he becáme my <u>saviour</u>.
   With joy you wíll draw <u>water</u>
   from the wells óf sal<u>va</u>tion. ℟.

2 Give thanks tó the <u>Lord</u>,
   give praise tó his <u>name</u>!
   Make his mighty deeds known tó the <u>peoples</u>,
   declare the greatness óf his <u>name</u>. ℟.

3 Sing a psalm to the Lord
   for he has done gloríous <u>deeds</u>,
   make them known to áll the <u>earth</u>!
   People of Zion, sing and shóut for <u>joy</u>
   for great in your midst is the Holy Óne of <u>Israel</u>. ℟.

251G After 6th Reading (Psalm 18(19))

Response

You have the mes - sage of e - ter - nal life, O Lord.

1 The law of the Lórd is <u>perfect</u>,
   it revíves the <u>soul</u>.
   The rule of the Lord is tó be <u>trusted</u>,
   it gives wisdom tó the <u>simple</u>. ℟.

2 The precepts of the Lórd are <u>right</u>,
   they gladdén the <u>heart</u>.
   The command of the Lórd is <u>clear</u>,
   it gives light tó the <u>eyes</u>. ℟.

3 The fear of the Lórd is <u>holy</u>,
   abidíng for <u>ever</u>.
   The decrees of the Lórd are the <u>truth</u>
   and all óf them <u>just</u>. ℟.

4 They are more to be desíred than <u>gold</u>,
   than the purést <u>gold</u>
   and sweeter are théy than <u>honey</u>,
   than honey fróm the <u>comb</u>. ℟.

251H After 7th Reading (Psalms 41(42) and 42(43))

Response

Like the deer that yearns for run - ning streams,—— so my soul is yearn - ing for you, my God.——

D   Bm⁷   G   Em⁷   A⁷sus   A⁷
C   C maj⁷   B   Am⁷   D

1 My soul is thirstíng for God,
the God óf my life;
when can I entér and see
(⸲) the fáce of God?   ℞.

2 These things will I remember
as I pour óut my soul:
how I would lead the rejoicing crowd
into the hóuse of God,
amid cries of gladness ánd thanksgiving,
the throng wíld with joy.   ℞.

3 O send forth your light ánd your truth;
let these bé my guide.
Let them bring me to your hóly mountain
to the place whére you dwell.   ℞.

4 And I will come to the altár of God,
the God óf my joy.
My redeemer, I will thank you ón the harp,
(⸲) O Gód, my God.   ℞.

251I Alternative Psalm after 7th Reading, especially when there is to be a baptism (Psalm 50(51))

For another alternative use 251F, especially when there is to be a baptism.

1 A pure heart create for mé, O <u>God</u>,
   put a steadfast spirít with<u>in</u> me.
   Do not cast me away fróm your <u>presence</u>,
   nor deprive me of your hóly <u>spirit</u>. ℟.

2 Give me again the joy óf your <u>help</u>;
   with a spirit of fervóur sus<u>tain</u> me,
   that I may teach transgressórs your <u>ways</u>
   and sinners may retúrn to <u>you</u>. ℟.

3 For in sacrifice you take nó de<u>light</u>,
   burnt offering from me you wóuld re<u>fuse</u>,
   my sacrifice, a cóntrite <u>spirit</u>.
   A humbled, contrite heart you wíll not <u>spurn</u>. ℟.

251J After New Testament Reading (Psalm 117(118))

(Alternatively, the tone for the preceding psalms could be repeated.)

1 Give thanks to the Lord for hé is <u>good</u>,
 for his love hás no <u>end</u>.
 Let the sons of Ísrael <u>say</u>:
 "His love hás no <u>end</u>." ℟.

2 The Lord's right hánd has tr<u>iu</u>mphed;
 his right hand ráised me <u>up</u>.
 I shall not die, Í shall <u>live</u>
 and recóunt his <u>deeds</u>. ℟.

3 The stone which the buildérs re<u>jec</u>ted
 has become the córner <u>stone</u>.
 This is the work óf the <u>Lord</u>,
 a marvel ín our <u>eyes</u>. ℟.

252 Easter Vigil: Baptismal Acclamation

David Kingsley

For use as the Paschal Candle is withdrawn from the water during the Blessing of Water.

Other verses may be composed.

253 Easter Sequence

Words: *Michael Hodgetts*
Music: *Chris McCurry*

Joyfully

All: 1 The Pa - schal Lamb is sac - ri - ficed,— the
Men: 2 For Death and Life fought hand - to - hand,— a
Solo Woman: 3 ׳ On - ly the shroud and cloths were there— in
Women: 4 And then I saw the Lord who died:— he
All: 5 Yes, all is true that Ma - ry said,— for

ran - somed sheep ex - ult in Christ:— now God and man are
du - el hard to un - der - stand,— and Life was killed but
side the em - pty se - pul - chre,— but tes - ti - fy - ing
is a - live and glo - ri - fied;— I saw my hope, whom
Christ has ri - sen from the dead.— Lord, reign as our im -

re - con - ciled,— the guil - ty by the un - de - filed.—
lives to reign:— now, Ma - ry, tell the Church a - gain.—
an - gels said— that Christ had ri - sen from the dead.—
you will see— when you re - turn to Ga - li - lee.—
mor - tal King,— and use your power for par - don - ing.—

254 Easter Song: You sons and daughters of the Lord

Text taken from "O filii et filiae"
Vs 1–4 trans. Edward Caswall,
revised by Robert Sherlaw Johnson
Vs 5–6 trans. Robert Sherlaw Johnson
Music: Robert Sherlaw Johnson

day him-self— from death re-stored.} AL - LE - LU - IA. 2 ALL
SEE THE TOMB— WHERE JE - SUS LAY. }

-IA.   3 Of spi - ces pure a pre-cious store in their pure hands— those
STRAIGHTWAY ONE IN WHITE THEY SEE, WHO SAYS: "YOU SEEK— THE

wo-men bore, to a-noint— the sa - cred bo-dy o'er. } AL - LE - LU - IA.   4 THEN
LORD; BUT HE— IS RISEN, AND GONE TO GA-LI-LEE". }

-IA.   Al - le-lu - ia, al - le-lu - ia, AL - LE - LU - IA.   5 May

he from whom__ all bless - ings flow his bless - ing now__ on us be - stow; Be-
GLO - RY TO__ OUR HEAVEN - LY KING, IN HEA - VEN LET__ OUR PRAI - SES RING, NOW

(as before)

ne - di - ca - mus Do - mi - no. } AL - LE - LU - IA.   6 ALL
"DE - O GRA - TI - AS" WE SING. }

All

1   *Congr.*

f   *mf*

+8va - - - - - - - - - - - - - - - - - - -

2   *Choir*   *Choir S/T*   *rit.*

Choir A/B and Congr.

-IA.   Al - le - lu - ia,   AL - LE - LU - IA.

rit.

235

Part VI · Weddings

255 O blessed are those
(Psalm 127(128):1–2,3,4–5)

Paul Inwood

Note: Psalm 127(128) is also the Responsorial Psalm for the Feast of the Holy Family and for 33 Sunday Year A.

Lord and walk in his ways! By the la-bour of your hands you shall
vine in the heart of your house; your chil-dren like shoots of the
blest all those who fear the Lord. May the Lord bless you from

F#m⁷ Bm⁷ Em⁷ A⁷ D add 9 D Dmaj⁷ G Em⁶
(Em⁷) (Am⁷) (Dm⁷) (G⁷) (C add 9) (C)(Cmaj⁷) (F) (Dm⁶)

eat. You will be hap - py and pros - per. O
ol - ive a - round your ta - ble. O
Zi - on all the days of your life! O

F#m⁷ Bm⁷ Em⁷ A sus 4 A⁷
(Em⁷) (Am⁷) (Dm⁷) (G sus 4) (G⁷)

D.S.

256 Psalm 32(33)   *Andrew J Mackriell*

(♩ = 92)

All (first time Cantor / Choir, All repeat)

Refrain May your love,   may your love   be up -

May your love be up - on us, may your love be up -

D Dmaj⁷ Em/D D A/C#

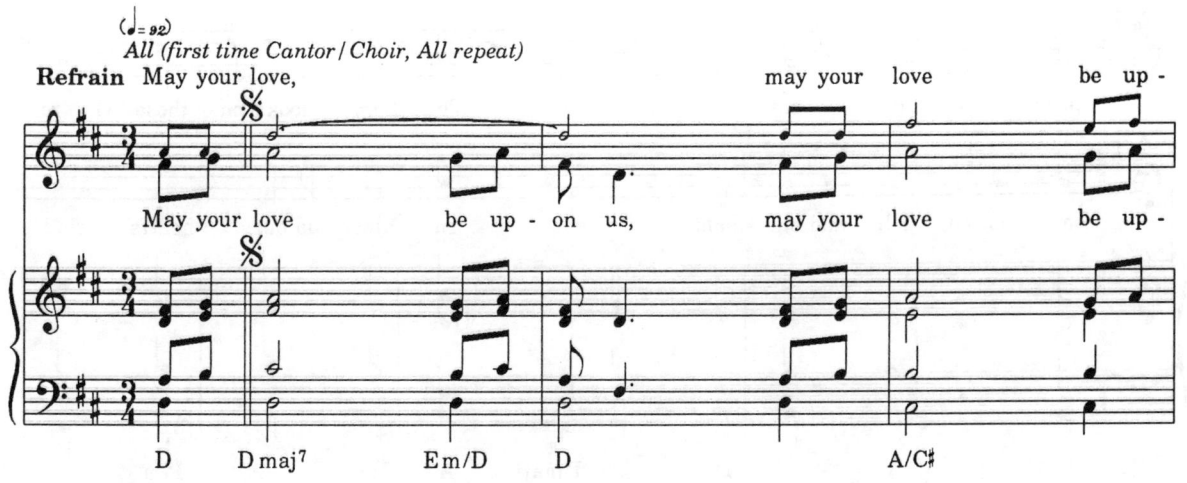

on us as we place all our hope in you.

on us as we place all our hope in you._____

Bm   Bm/A   F   Gsus 2   G   D

Cantor/Choir
Verses

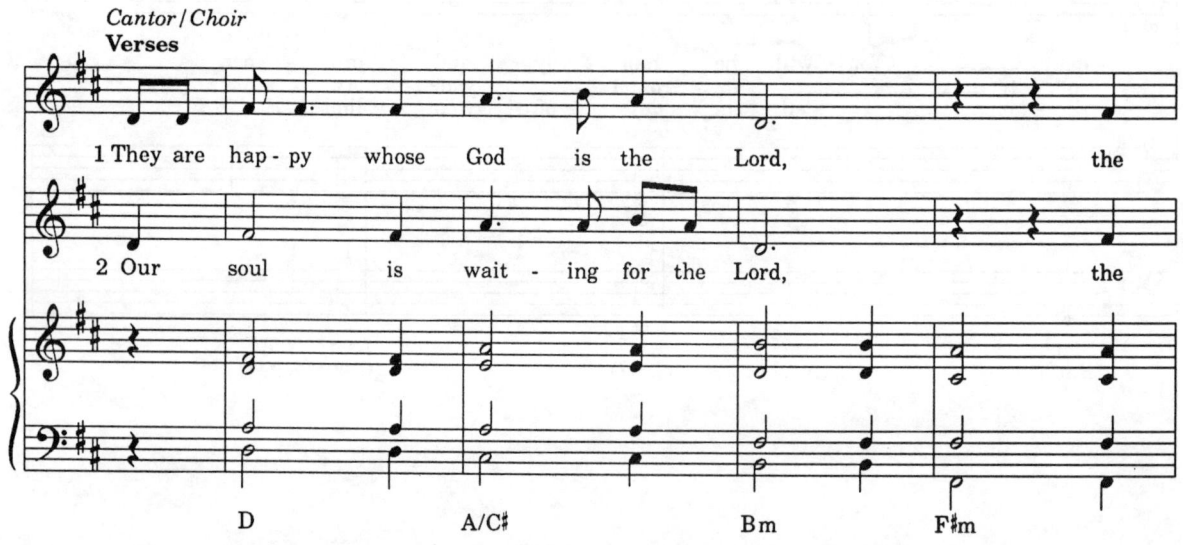

1 They are hap-py whose God is the Lord, the

2 Our soul is wait-ing for the Lord, the

D   A/C#   Bm   F#m

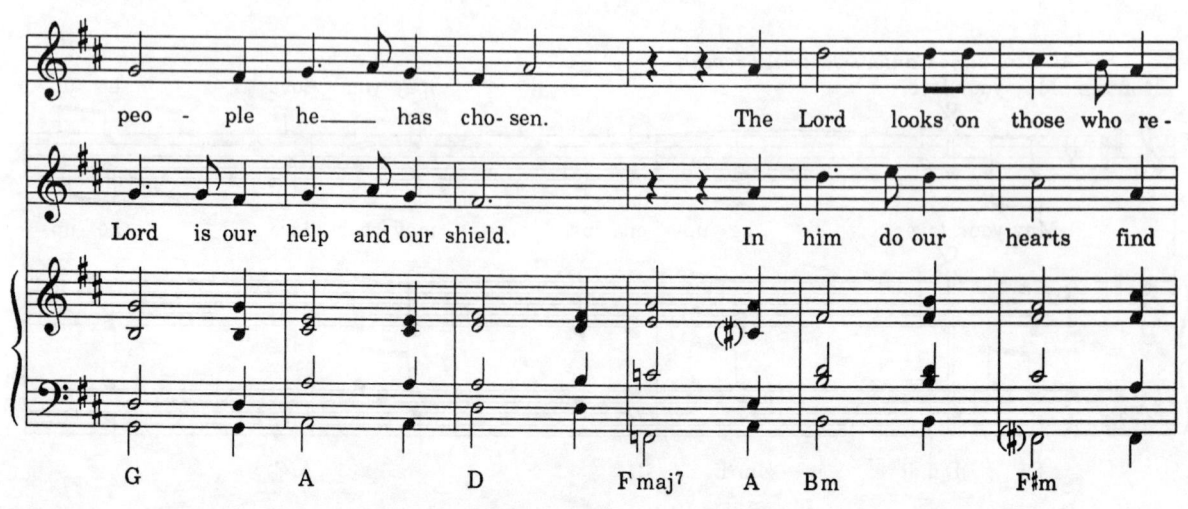

peo-ple he___ has cho-sen. The Lord looks on those who re-

Lord is our help and our shield. In him do our hearts find

G   A   D   Fmaj7   A   Bm   F#m

238

vere him, on those who hope in his love._____ May your

joy_____ we trust in his ho - ly name._____ May your

Gsus 2 G A F G A9sus4 A

257 Alleluia for Marriages: God is love

Gerry Fitzpatrick

Response

Al - le - lu - ia, al - le - lu - ia, al - le - lu - ia, al - le - lu - ia.

D G A D Bm Em7 A D

Verse

Al - le - lu - ia, al - le - lu - ia, God__ is love, let us love one an - o - ther.

G A F♯m Bm Em7 A D

Al - le - lu - ia, al - le - lu - ia, let__ us love__ as God has loved us.

G A F♯m Bm Em7 A D

239

258 The Bridegroom's Song

Text: Patrick Lee
Music: Philip Gaisford

Unison

1 The win-ter time on earth shall pass and tear-ful rains shall cease;
the prom-ised flow-ers come to bloom, a dove shall her-ald peace.
Then love shall clothe, then love shall clothe my Word with flesh.

2 No lily set among the thorns
has beauty like my Love's;
her eyes, half seen behind her veil,
gleam soft as any dove's.
This love shall clothe my Word with flesh.

3 A single glance can wound my heart,
a strand of hair set free
can bind that heart to her whose love
is more than wine to me.
Such love shall clothe my Word with flesh.

4 Her lips are scarlet like the thread,
her voice like lilting song,
her gentle kisses taste like milk
and honey on the tongue.
And love shall clothe my Word with flesh.

5 My Bride, a garden by a stream
with rows of cypress trees,
has lovelier fragrance than their scent
when stirred by evening breeze.
Now love shall clothe my Word with flesh.

6 Her beauty's brighter than the sun,
the moon is not so fair;
her perfume, as she moves abroad,
is frankincense and myrrh.
Her love shall clothe my Word with flesh.

259 Bridegroom and Bride

Text: The Iona Community
Music: trad. Irish, harmony M Shaw,
descant Geoffrey Boulton Smith

1 God, in the planning and purpose of life,
  Hallowed the union of husband and wife:
  This we embody where love is displayed,
  Rings are presented and promises made.

2 Jesus was found, at a similar feast,
  Taking the roles of both waiter and priest,
  Turning the worldly towards the divine,
  Tears into laughter and water to wine.

3 Therefore we pray that his spirit preside
  Over the wedding of bridegroom and bride,
  Fulfilling all that they've hoped will come true,
  Lighting with love all they dream of and do.

4 Praise then the Maker, the Spirit, the Son,
  Source of the love through which two are made one.
  God's is the glory, the goodness and grace
  Seen in this marriage and known in this place.

260 Jesus, stand among us

Matthew 18:20

Graham Kendrick

With warmth

1 Je - sus, stand a - mong us___ at the meet - ing of our lives,

Capo 3 E♭ (C)   Fm (Dm)   B♭7 (G7)   E♭ (C)

be our sweet a - gree - ment at the meet - ing of our eyes; O,

Fm (Dm)   B♭7 (G7)   E♭ (C)

Je - sus, we love You, so we ga - ther here,

A♭ (F)   Gm (Em)   A♭ (F)   Gm (Em)

1st time

join our hearts in un - i - ty___ and take a - way___ our

A♭ (F)   Gm (Em)   Fm (Dm)

242

2 So to You we're gathering
   Out of each and every land,
   Christ the love between us
   At the joining of our hands;
   O, Jesus, we love You. . . (etc.)

   (Optional verse for communion)

3 Jesus, stand among us
   At the breaking of the bread,
   Join us as one body
   As we worship You, our Head.
   O, Jesus, we love You. . . (etc.)

261 Psalm 129(130): Come to me

Noel Donnelly

2 Love and mercy flow from you,
   Lord of life and kind redeemer.

3 In the dark I hope for you,
   you are light of new day dawning.

4 Weak and frail we come to you,
   God of love and new beginning.

262 Song of Farewell

Text: Patrick Lee
Music: Philip Gaisford

2 Christ, who died, now reigns in triumph,
Christ has risen from the dead;
He has promised life for ever,
Follow where the Lord has led.

3 Christ returned from earth to heaven,
There he has prepared your place;
In his presence, with the Father,
Live in lasting light and peace.

4 Through the Lord you sought salvation,
In the Lord you placed your trust,
To the Lord you gave your service,
With the Lord find holy rest.

263 This is my friend

Anthony Hemson

knew, he was there to lift me up a-gain!——What more can friend - ship do?——

2 Life's distractions made me think I'd seen
A way that led to deeper happiness.
But I learned that Christ is my redeemer
Who leads to paradise.

3 I have felt his hand upon my shoulder
Guiding me along the path of right.
Now my eyes have seen my Lord and master
To be my guiding light.

Choral Chorus

p

This is my friend with whom I shall spend all my days in——(in)
This is my friend with

won-der, love and praise.—— He knows my ways yet
He knows my
yet

to Verses | *Fine*
ppp

as a friend he stays be-side me un - til—— the end.——
be - side me un - til——

264 Processional Song: May the angels lead you

Howard Hughes SM

ci - ty, the new and e - ter - nal Je - ru - sa - lem.

Cantor / Choir

May the choir of an - gels wel-come you where

Laz - a - rus is poor no long - er, may you have e - ter - nal rest,

may you have e - ter - nal rest.

265 Requiem Chant

G Paul Johnstone

The Refrain should be repeated ad lib. with instrumental improvisations. Simple accompaniment only should be used for the solo verses. It is not necessary for each solo verse to be sung straight after the previous one; it may be preferable to repeat the Refrain between verses.

266 Ag Críost an síol
(To Christ the seed)

Text: trad. Irish, trans. JW
Music: Sean Ó Riada

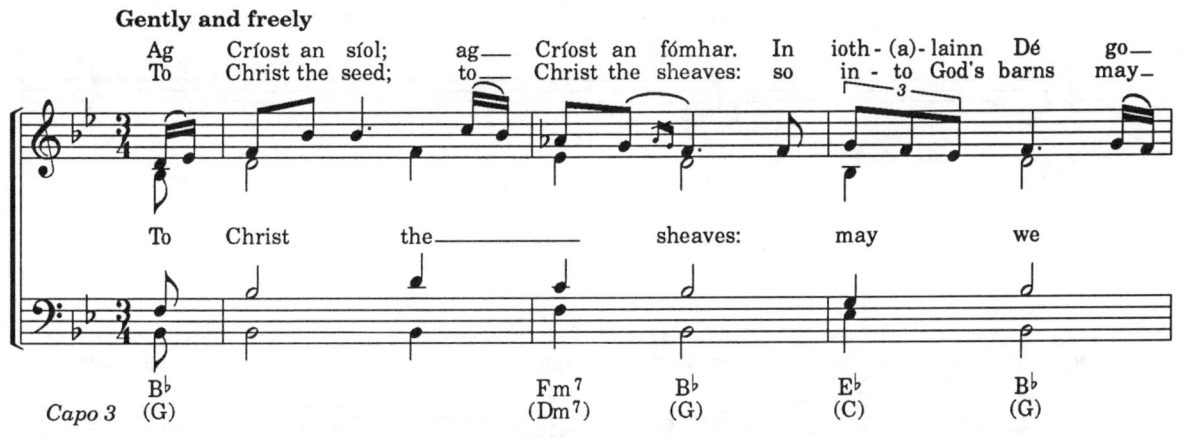

Gently and freely

Ag Críost an síol; ag— Críost an fómhar. In ioth-(a)-lainn Dé go—
To Christ the seed; to— Christ the sheaves: so in-to God's barns may—

To Christ the——— sheaves: may we

Capo 3 (G)   Bb (G)   Fm⁷ (Dm⁷)   Bb (G)   Eb (C)   Bb (G)

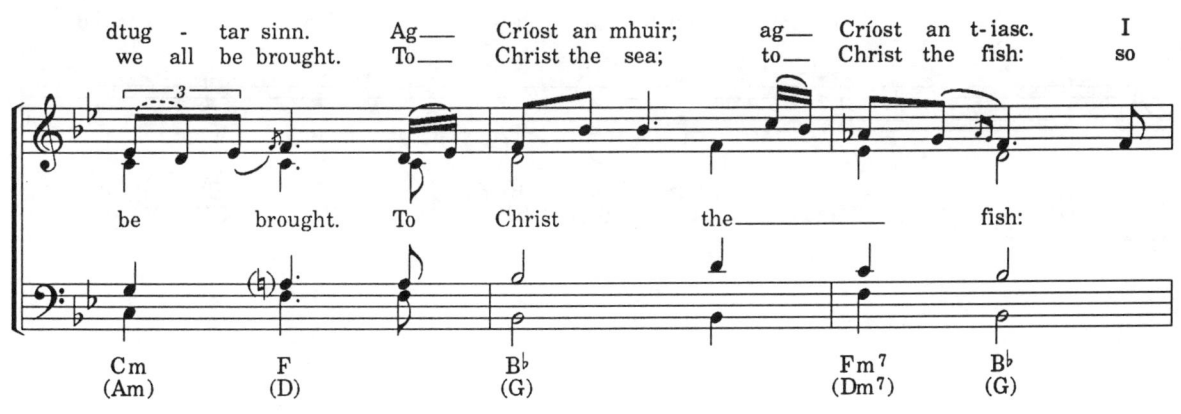

dtug-tar sinn. Ag— Críost an mhuir; ag— Críost an t-iasc. I
we all be brought. To— Christ the sea; to— Christ the fish: so

be brought. To Christ the——— fish:

Cm (Am)   F (D)   Bb (G)   Fm⁷ (Dm⁷)   Bb (G)

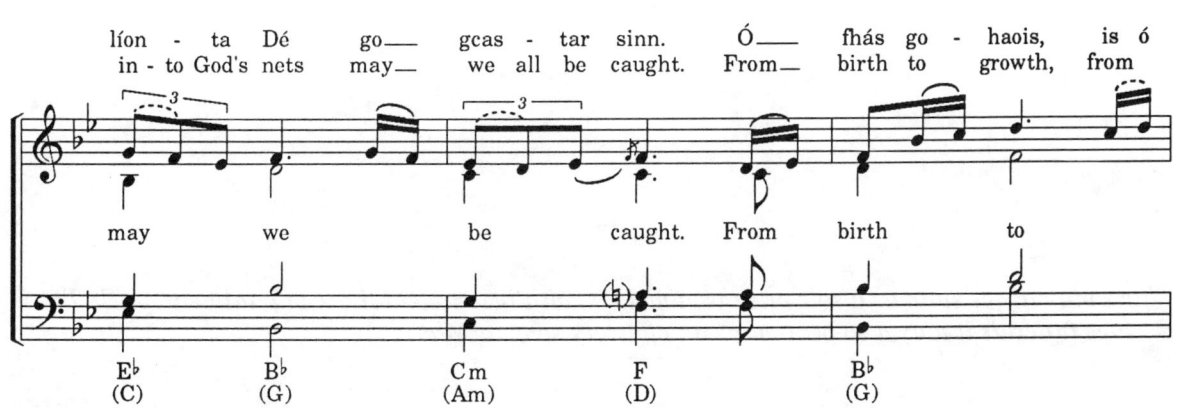

líon-ta Dé go— gcas-tar sinn. Ó— fhás go-haois, is ó
in-to God's nets may— we all be caught. From— birth to growth, from

may we be caught. From birth to

Eb (C)   Bb (G)   Cm (Am)   F (D)   Bb (G)

251

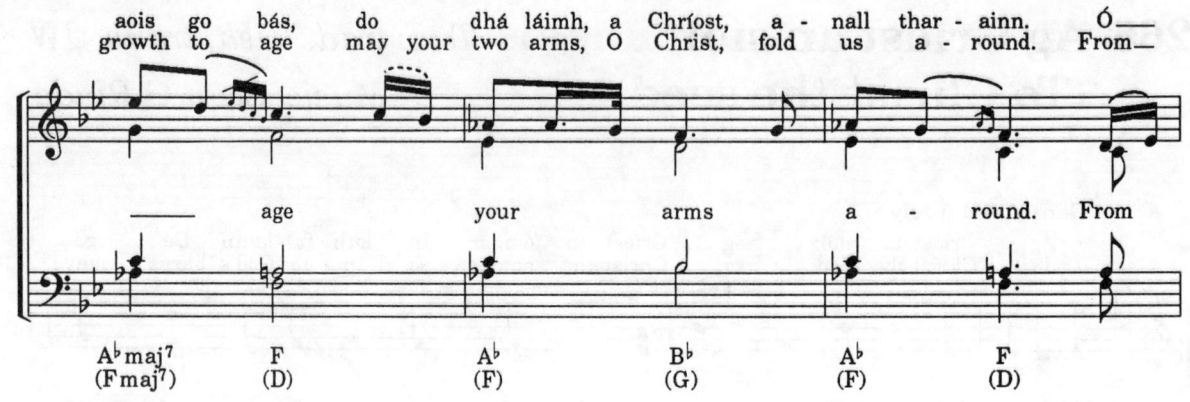

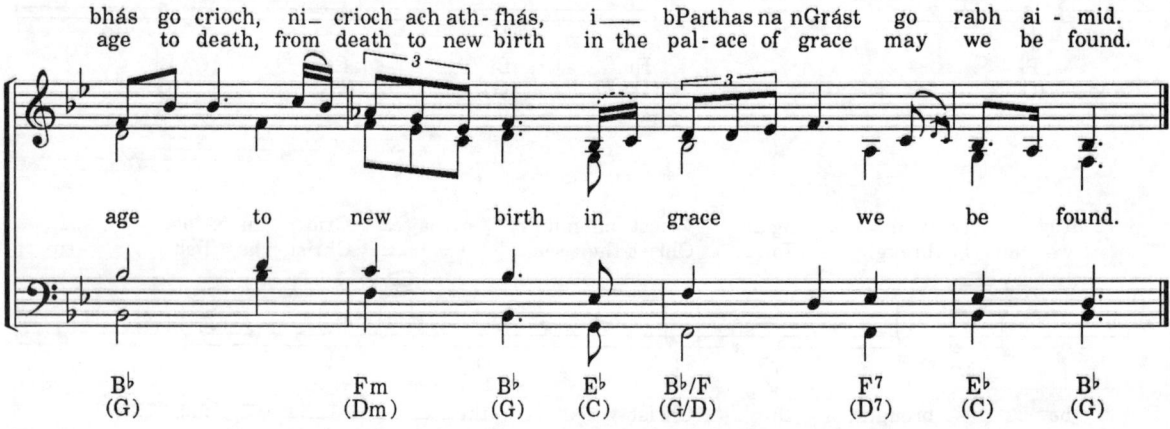

This song may be sung as a solo or unison melody with instrumental accompaniment, or SATB.
Besides funerals it may also be used as an offertory song at Mass.

267 May the choirs of angels

Ernest Sands

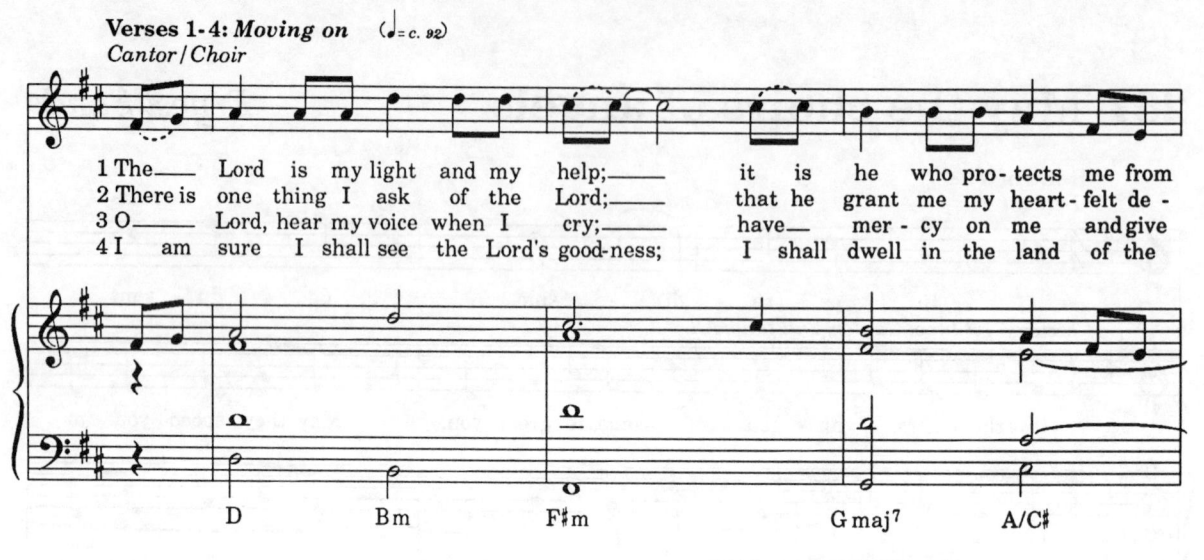

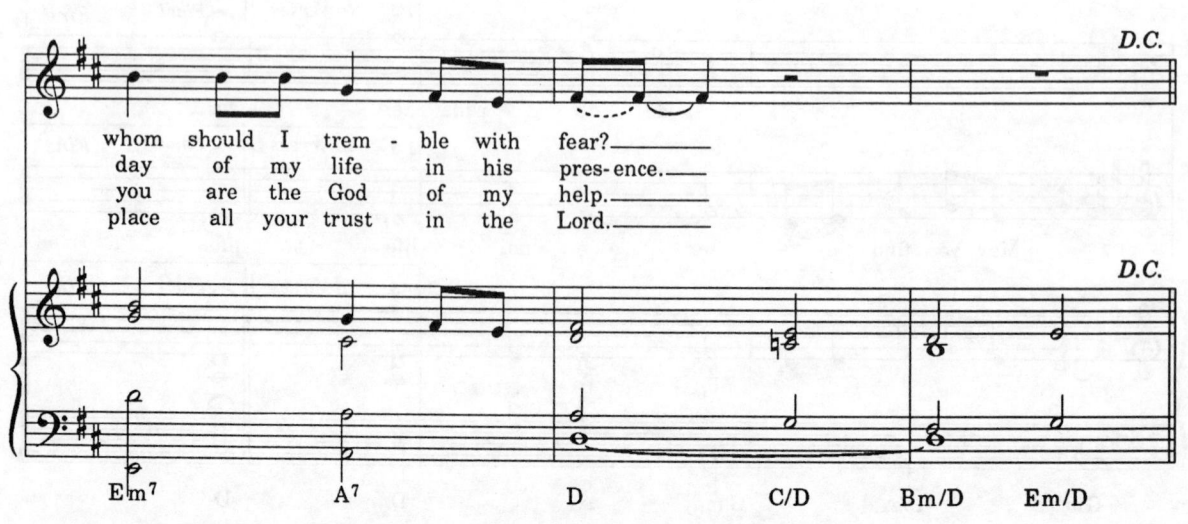

254

268 The Lord is my light
Jacques Berthier

from Psalm 26(27)

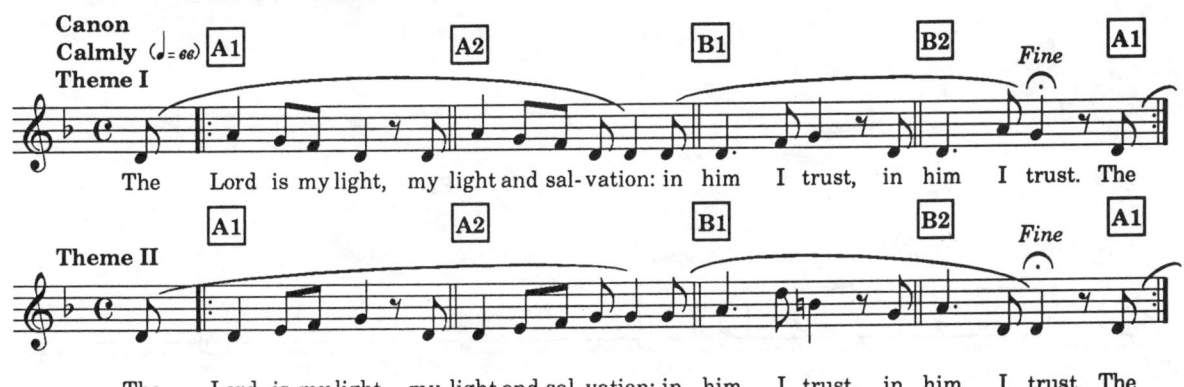

The Lord is my light, my light and sal-vation: in him I trust, in him I trust. The

The Lord is my light, my light and sal-vation: in him I trust, in him I trust. The

Each of the two themes can be sung separately *either* **in unison** *or* **as a round** *(two voices only: coming in on A1 and B1) The two themes can also be sung* together, *preferably with theme I for female voices and theme II for male voices.*

269 Praise the Lord from the heavens (Psalm 148)

Stephen Dean

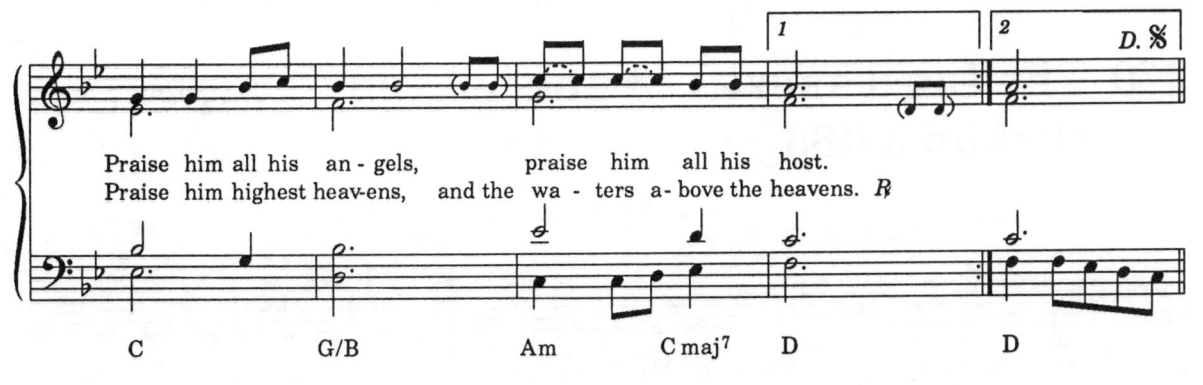

Praise him all his an-gels, praise him all his host.
Praise him highest heav-ens, and the wa-ters a-bove the heavens. ℞

C   G/B   Am   C maj⁷ D   D

Choral harmony for verses (sung in pairs between repetitions of Refrain)

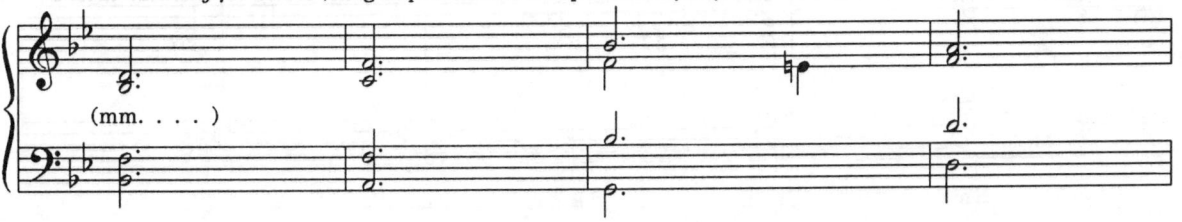

(mm. . . .)

2   *Let them práise the name of the Lórd. He commánded: they were máde.
      He fíxed them for éver, gave a láw which shall not pass awáy.
      Práise the Lord from the éarth, séa creatures and all óceans;
      fíre and hail, snow and míst, stormy wínds that obey his wórd.   ℞.

3   Áll mountains and hílls, áll fruit trees and cédars,
      béasts, wild and táme, réptiles and birds that flý.
      Áll earth's kings and péoples, earth's prínces and rúlers;
      yóung men and máidens, óld men, yes, and chíldren. ℞.

4   *Let them práise the name of the Lórd for hé alone is exálted.
      The spléndour of his náme goes beyónd heaven and éarth,
      He exálts the strength of his péople. He is the práise of all his sáints,
      of the péople of Israel, of the ónes he chooses for his ówn. ℞.

Extra syllables before first beat.

270 The Lord speaks of peace (Psalm 84(85))

Stephen Dean

hear what the Lord God is say - ing,_____ he brings us a
Just - ice and peace walk to - ge - ther,_____ (-) mer - cy has
Lord will pour bles - sings u - pon us;_____ the land will yield

A⁷   D   Em⁷

mes - sage of peace;_____ peace for his own faith - ful
joined hands with love;_____ faith - ful - ness springs up in
har - vests of grain._____ Jus - tice shall march on be -

A⁷   D   Dm   G⁷

D.C.

peo - ple,_____ if on - ly they turn and take heed._____
blos - som,_____ and jus - tice looks down from a - bove._____
fore him,_____ pre - pa - ring the way for his reign._____

D.C.

C   C maj⁷   Am/C   F♯7sus4   F♯7

259

271 Holy Spirit of God, teach us to love   *Ray d'Inverno*

260

272 Veni, veni, Sancte Spiritus
(Spirit hov'ring o'er the waters)

Noel Donnelly

Spi - rit hov -'ring o'er the wa - ters, — when the world from cha - os — be - gan,

Capo 1 (D) E♭ (D)   A♭ (G)   E♭ (D)   Cm (Bm)   E♭ (D)   A♭ (G)   E♭ (D)   B♭ (A)

Liv - ing Spi - rit, re - cre - ate us! — Come, re - store our hearts with life.

E♭ (D)   A♭ (G)   Gm (F♯m)   E♭ (D)   D♭ (C)   E♭ (D)

Choir double organ parts

Ve - ni, ve - ni, San - cte Spi - ri - tus,

E♭ (D)   B♭ (A)   Cm (Bm)   G (F♯)   Cm (Bm)   A♭ (G)   Fm (Em)   B♭ (A)   E♭ (D)

2 Spirit speaking through the prophets
   when they cried for justice and peace,
   Living Spirit, come renew us,
   fill the earth with peace and love. ℟.

3 Spirit hov'ring o'er the virgin,
   Word and flesh are mothered in her.
   Living Spirit, breath of Yahweh,
   bring the Word to life in us. ℟.

4 Spirit breathed on John and Mary
   as they stood there under the cross,
   Living Spirit, strengthen, comfort,
   guide, unite your church today. ℟.

5 Spirit hov'ring o'er apostles,
   wind and fire of Pentecost Day,
   Living Spirit, now confirm us,
   come inspire us, come, we pray. ℟.

273 Song of Resurrection

Patrick Geary

God has en-lightened our minds to see the hope of his call.
called out of dark-ness; called to live in God's won-der-ful light.
We are no long-er slaves but heirs to the Kingdom of God,

Db Bb7   Eb   Cm   Fm   Ab   Bbsus   Bb/Ab   2

cresc.

We are the light of the world. Let our light shine out, so that
Sing to the glo-ry of God; let your praise ring out, so that
filled with the Spi-rit of Christ tell the world "Je-sus is Lord!" so that

G   G/F   Cm/Eb   Cm   G   C   G   Bm

God's sal-va-tion may reach the ends of the earth.
God's sal-va-tion may reach the ends of the earth.
God's sal-va-tion may reach the ends of the earth.

D.S.

Am   G/B   Am/C   Em   Am7   C   Dsus   D

264

Treble instrument

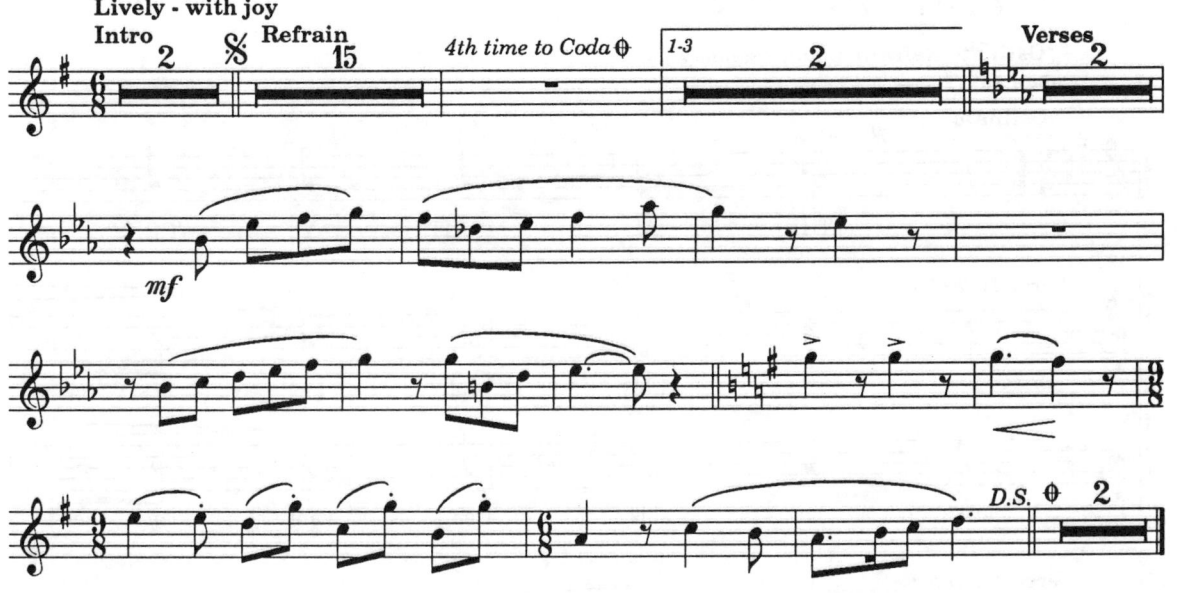

B flat Trumpet

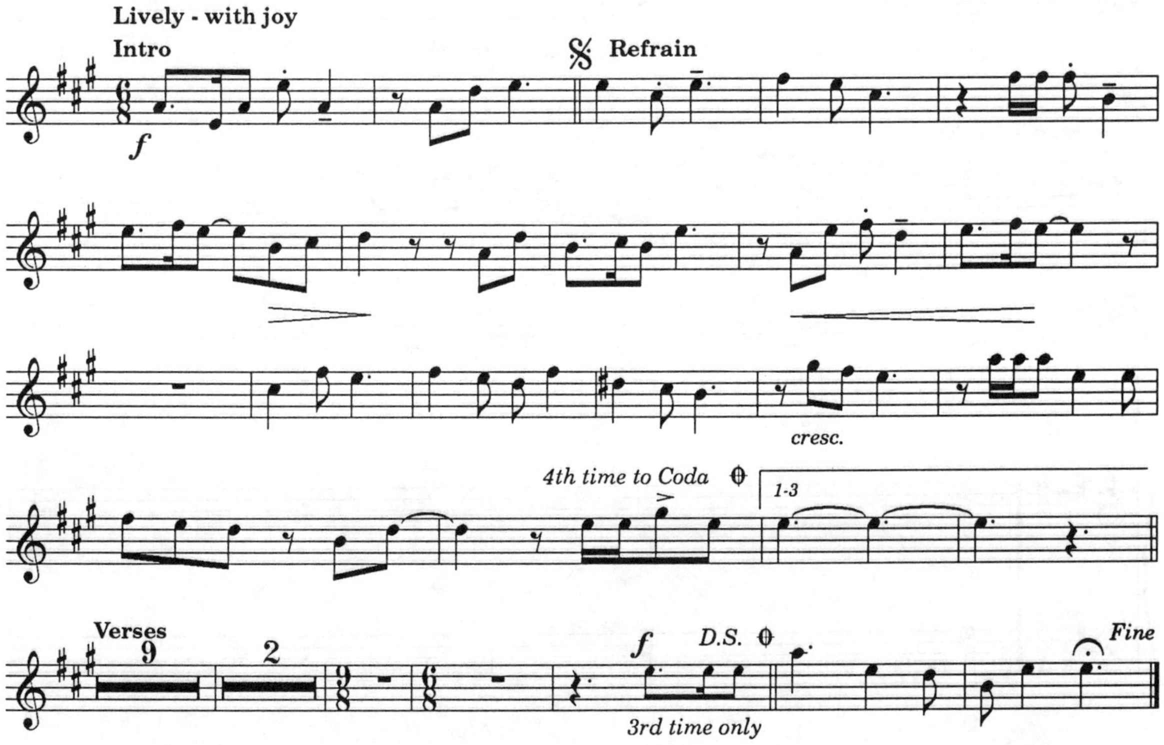

274 Magnificat

Peter Jones

Based on Luke 1:46–55

*Ostinato Refrain: *Choir, Assembly*

Gently (♩ = c. 76)

Ostinato

p

THE   AL -   MIGHT - Y   WORKS

Verse 1: *Cantor*

mp

1 My   soul   glo - ri - fies   the

looks   on   his   ser - vant   in her

Verse 2: *Cantor*

mp

2 His   mer - cy   is   from

mf

puts   forth——   his   arm   in   strength   and

Verse 3: *Cantor*

mp

3 He   pro - tects   Is - ra - el,   re -

chil - dren   for   ev - er.

p

D   A/C♯

*Sing twice at beginning and ending of piece, once between verses.

MAR - VELS FOR ME. HO - LY HIS

Lord. My spi - rit re -

low - li - ness;_____ hence - forth all

age to age;_____ on those who

scat - ters____ the proud____ heart - ed; he casts the might - y

mem - b'ring his mer - cy, as he prom - ised to our

p

Al - le -

Bm A⁶ G maj⁷

NAME, HOLY HIS NAME.

(∩) Fine

1 joic - es in God my Sav - iour. He
mp

a - ges will call me blest.
to Refrain then V2

2 fear him, on those who fear him he

down and rais - es the low - ly.
to Refrain then V3

3 fa - thers to A - bra - ham and his
to Refrain al Fine

lu - ia.

(Fine)

D/F♯   Em⁷   A⁹   A

Chimes

Gently (♩ = c. 76)
Refrain: Tacet   **Verse 1: Tacet**   ***Refrain**

16   16

p

Verses 2,3: Tacet
(Fine)   16   D.S.

275 World without end

The Iona Community
Music: Scottish trad.

With a stately rhythm

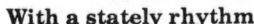

Capo 3 (D)

F
(D)

Gm⁷
(Em⁷)

C
(A)

F
(D)

Dm
(Bm)

Am
(F♯m)

B♭⁹
(G⁹)

Am⁷
(F♯m⁷)

F
(D)

B♭
(G)

Gm⁷
(Em⁷)

F/A
(D/F♯)

B♭maj⁷
(Gmaj⁷)

C
(A)

1   Praise to the Lord for the joys of the earth:
    Cycles of season and reason and birth,
    Contrasts in outlook and landscape and need,
    Challenge of famine, pollution and greed.

2   Praise to the Lord for the progress of life:
    Cradle and grave, bond of husband and wife,
    Pain of youth growing and wrinkling of age,
    Questions in step with experience and stage.

3   Praise to the Lord for his care of our kind:
    Faith for the faithless and sight for the blind,
    Healing, acceptance, disturbance and change,
    All the emotions through which our lives range.

4   Praise to the Lord for the people we meet,
    Safe in our homes or at risk in the street:
    Kiss of a lover and friendship's embrace,
    Smile of a stranger and words full of grace.

5   Praise to the Lord for the carpenter's son,
    Dovetailing worship and work into one:
    Tradesman and teacher and vagrant and friend,
    Source of all life in this world without end.

276 God is good

Graham Kendrick

Ps 99(100):5; Heb 4:16

277 Shine, Jesus, shine
(Lord, the light of Your love)

Graham Kendrick

... fill this land with the Fa-ther's glo-ry: blaze, Spi-rit, blaze,— set our

A Bm Bm/A Esus4 E A E/A A D A
(G) (Am)(Am7) (Dsus4) (D) (G) (D) (G) (C) (G)

hearts on fire. Flow, ri-ver, flow,— flood the na-tions with

Bm Bm/A G Esus4 E A E/A A D A Bm Bm/A
(Am) (Am7) (F) (Dsus4)(D) (G) (D) (G) (C) (G) (Am) (Am7)

grace and mer-cy; send forth Your Word,— Lord, and let there be

Esus4 E A E/A A D A Bm E7
(Dsus4) (D) (G) (D) (G) (C) (G) (Am) (D7)

Last time

light. *rit.*

A D/A E/A D/A A D/A A
(G) (C) (D) (C) (G) (C) (G)

2 Lord, I come to Your awesome presence,
From the shadows into Your radiance;
By the blood I may enter Your brightness.
Search me, try me, consume all my darkness.
Shine on me, shine on me.

3 As we gaze on Your kingly brightness
So our faces display Your likeness,
Ever changing from glory to glory.
Mirrored here may our lives tell Your story.
Shine on me, shine on me.

(Chorus twice to end.)

278 Irish Blessing

Lizzy Ann Dunworth

May the road rise up to meet you.___ May the wind be al - ways at your

back.___ May the sun shine warm upon your face,___ and the

rain fall soft u - pon your fields.___ And un - til we

meet a-gain,_____ may God hold you, may God hold you,

D⁹ D Gm D Fmaj⁷ G

Repeat ad lib. | *Last time* *Fine*

hold you in the palm of his hand._____ May the hand._____

f *mp* *pp*

Fmaj⁷ Em/G A⁷sus4 A⁷ A⁷sus4 D

cresc.

Acknowledgements

Every effort has been made to trace copyright holders but should there be any inadvertent errors or omissions in this list, the publishers offer their sincere apologies and will rectify any mistakes in future editions.

The publishers wish to thank the following for permission to use copyright material in this collection:

Robert Adams, 69 Charlton Church Lane, London SE7 7AB, for the music of *195 All the gifts of God are holy.*

John Ainslie, 76 Great Bushey Drive, Totteridge, London N20 8QL, for the music of *167 The Barnet Gloria* © John Ainslie 1989, *200 Holy, holy* © John Ainslie 1991 and *225 Bread of the world* © John Ainslie 1991.

Mike Anderson, 11a Rampit Close, Penny Lane, Haydock, Merseyside WA11 0YH, for the music of *168 Gloria.*

Tony Barr, 784 Riverwood Drive, Keizer, OR 97303, USA, for the music of *175 Alleluia.* Reprinted by permission of Jabulani Music, © Tony Barr 1976.

Liam Bauress, Worth School, Worth Abbey, Turners Hill, Crawley, West Sussex RH10 4SD, for the music of *192 Music for the Intercessions* and *201 Eucharistic Acclamations.*

Geoffrey Boulton Smith, 66 Belmont Road, Portswood, Southampton, Hants SO2 1GE, for the music of *176 Alleluia for many Sundays, 218 Lamb of God, 226 In praise of Christ, 245 Good Friday: Responsorial Psalm, 246 This is the wood of the cross* and *249 Exsultet.*

Peter Clark, 7 Wordsworth Avenue, Roath, Cardiff CF2 1AQ, for the text and music of *154 Into your presence.*

Michael Coy, 120 Hornchurch Road, Hornchurch, Essex RM11 1DL, for the music of *196 A Christmas Offertory.*

Mrs Catherine Dalal, Oakenroode, Oakenrod Hill, Rochdale, Lancs, for the music of *174 Alleluias* and *232 Hymn for Christian Unity* by Harold Barker, © Mrs Catherine Dalal.

Stephen Dean, 30 North Terrace, Mildenhall, Suffolk IP28 7AB, for the music of *162 Lord, have mercy* and *197 Preparation of the Gifts* from *A Short Mass for Advent and Lent; 177 Easter Acclamation, 202 St Andrew's Responsorial Acclamations, 269 Praise the Lord from the heavens* and *270 The Lord speaks of peace.* All © Stephen Dean. Published by Oregon Catholic Press, 5536 NE Hassalo, Portland, OR 97213, USA. Administered in UK by Calamus, 30 North Terrace, Mildenhall, Suffolk IP28 7AB.

Ray d'Inverno, 26 Thornbury Avenue, Shirley, Southampton, Hants SO15 5BR, for the music of *169 Gloria* from *A Children's Mass, 238 Were we with you, Jesus?* and *271 Holy Spirit of God.*

Noel Donnelly, 80 Cardross Road, Dumbarton, Scotland G82 4JQ, for the music of *261 Psalm 129(130): Come to me* and *272 Spirit hov'ring o'er the waters.*

E A Dunworth, The Lay Community, Worth Abbey, Paddockhurst Road, Turners Hill, Crawley, West Sussex RH10 4SB, for the music of *278 Irish Blessing* © E A Dunworth 1990, printed by kind permission of McKeigne Enterprises, 9 Park Road, Cheadle, Cheshire SK8 2AN.

Bernadette Farrell, 36 Cameford Court, New Park Road, London SW2 4LH, for the music of *178 Praise to you, O Christ, our Saviour, 203 Holy, holy, Memorial Acclamation B* and *Amen* from *Eucharistic Acclamations* and *204 Eucharistic Acclamations for Children.* All © Bernadette Farrell. Published by Oregon Catholic Press, 5536 NE Hassalo, Portland, OR 97213, USA. Administered in UK by Calamus, 30 North Terrace, Mildenhall, Suffolk IP28 7AB.

276

Gerry Fitzpatrick, St Columba's, 74 Hopehill Road, Glasgow G20 7HH, for the music of *179 Alleluias: Stay awake, I am the way, Come Holy Spirit, 193 Lord turn to your people* and *257 God is love.*

Derek Fry, St John's RC Cathedral, Portsmouth PO1 3HG, for the music of *170 Gloria, 205 Holy, holy* and *219 Agnus Dei*, all from *Mass of St Edmund of Abingdon.*

Sue Furlong, 6 Tuskar View, Wexford, Ireland, for the music of *206 Eucharistic Acclamations* from *Eucharistic Prayer for Children* and *243 The blessing cup.*

Fr Philip Gaisford OSB, Worth Abbey, Paddockhurst Road, Turners Hill, Crawley, West Sussex RH10 4SB for the music of *171 "Gifts" Gloria, 180 Alleluia No. 3, 181 Alleluia No. 4, 258 The Bridegroom's Song* and *262 Song of Farewell* © Fr Philip Gaisford (Worth Abbey Music).

Paul Gardner, 73 The Hundred, Romsey, Hants SO51 8BZ, for the text of *238 Were we with you, Jesus?*

Patrick Geary, 17 Elmgrove Road, Cotham, Bristol BS6 6AH, for the music of *155 Listen to the voice of the Lord, 182 Gospel Acclamations for Lent, 220 Lamb of God* and *273 Song of Resurrection.*

GIA Publications Inc., 7404 South Mason Avenue, Chicago, Illinois 60638, USA, for the music of *156 Gather us in* and *227 Your love is finer than life (Psalm 62(63))* by Marty Haugen and *264 May the angels lead you* by Howard Hughes. All © GIA Publications Inc. Used by permission.

The Grail, England for texts of *187 Psalm 116(117), 188 Gospel Acclamation, 241 Psalm 21(22), 243 Responsorial Psalm 115(116), 245 Psalm 30(31), 255 O blessed are those* and *256 Psalm 32(33)* from *The Psalms: A New Translation* published by William Collins, Sons & Co Ltd (now HarperCollins Publishers); text of *199 The Grail Prayer.*

Rev Emmanuel Gribben, St Augustine's Presbytery, St Austin's Place, Preston PR1 3YJ, for the music of *183 Mantra Alleluia* and *233 Go now*, both from *Prayer and Praise.* Printed with permission of St Augustine's Pastoral Liturgy Centre, St Austin's Place, Preston PR1 3YJ.

Anthony Hemson, Director of Parish Music, Belmont Abbey, Hereford, for *263 This is my friend* in memory of B C H.

Michael Hodgetts, 68 Goldieslie Road, Sutton Coldfield, West Midlands B73 5PG, for the texts of *240 Entrance Antiphon: When Christ the King rode down the street* and *253 Easter Sequence* © Michael Hodgetts.

Rt Rev Crispian Hollis, Bishop of Portsmouth, Bishop's House, Edinburgh Road, Portsmouth PO1 3HG, for the text of *191 Creed: We believe, we believe.*

The House of the Open Door Community, Childswickham House, Childswickham, Broadway, Worcs WR12 7HH, for *214 Holy, holy* by Kevin Sumpter © HOD Community.

Bob Hurd and OCP Publications, PO Box 13248, Portland, OR 97213, USA, for the music of *228 As the deer longs*, © Bob Hurd and OCP Publications. All rights reserved. Used by permission.

ICEL (International Commission on English in the Liturgy), Suite 1202, 1275 K Street NW, Washington DC 20005, USA, for text of *264 May the angels lead you* from *Rite of Funerals* © 1970, International Commission on English in the Liturgy, Inc. (ICEL); excerpts from the English translation of *Rite of Holy Week* © 1970, ICEL; excerpts from the English translation of *The Roman Missal* ©1973, ICEL; music of *264 May the angels lead you* from *Music for the Rite of Funerals and Rite of Baptism for Children* © 1977, ICEL. All rights reserved.

Paul Inwood, 1195 E Fitzgerald, Simi Valley, CA 93065, USA, for *207 Eucharistic Acclamations* from *Gathering Mass: Holy, holy, Memorial Acclamation A, Memorial Acclamation B, Doxology and Amen, 221 Lamb of God,* all from *Gathering Mass,* printed with permission of OCP; *172 Gloria* from *Shrewsbury Mass, 247 Processional Song of the Cross, 248 O my people, 255 O blessed are those,* from *Lead me, O Lord* (OCP). All © Paul Inwood. Published by Oregon Catholic Press, 5536 NE Hassalo, Portland, OR 97213, USA. Administered in UK by Calamus, 30 North Terrace, Mildenhall, Suffolk IP28 7AB.

Iona Community, Wild Goose Publications, Pearce Institute, 840 Govan Road, Glasgow G51 3UT, for *157 Jesus calls us* from *Love from Below; 198 Among us and before us, 234 The Summons, 259 Bridegroom and Bride* and *275 World without end* from *Heaven Shall Not Wait,* © Wild Goose Publications/Iona Community, Glasgow, Scotland. Reproduced by permission.

Alan Johnson, 29 Sandcliffe Road, Wallasey, Wirral L45 3JH, for the music of *158 Entrance Song, Psalms 94(95)* and *103(104).*

Revd G Paul Johnstone, St Mary's Priory, Cleator, Cumbria CA23 3AB, for the music of *184 Alleluia: Easter Joy* and *265 Requiem Chant* from *Prayer and Praise.* Printed with permission of St Augustine's Pastoral Liturgy Centre, St Austin's Place, Preston PR1 3YJ.

Rev Peter Jones, St John Fisher, Tiverton Road, Wyken, Coventry CV2 3DL, for the music of *222 Lamb of God* and *274 Magnificat.* Published by Oregon Catholic Press, 5536 NE Hassalo, Portland, OR 97213, USA. Administered in UK by Calamus, 30 North Terrace, Mildenhall, Suffolk IP28 7AB.

Richard Jones, 65 Canford Lane, Westbury-on-Trym, Bristol BS9 3NX, for the music of *163 Penitential Rite 2.*

Feargal King, c/o Institute of Pastoral Liturgy, College St, Carlow, Ireland for the text and music of *235 King of All* © Feargal King and Toscaire Music 1991 and *159 Sing Gloria* © Feargal King and Toscaire Music 1990, and the music of *194 Prayers of the Faithful* © Feargal King and Toscaire Music 1990.

David Kingsley for the music of *252 Springs of water* © David Kingsley. Published by Oregon Catholic Press, 5536 NE Hassalo, Portland, OR 97213, USA. Administered in UK by Calamus, 30 North Terrace, Mildenhall, Suffolk IP28 7AB.

Patrick Lee, Mair Wen, 8 Hampton Fields, Oswestry, Salop SY11 1TJ, for the texts of *171 "Gifts" Gloria, 195 All the gifts of God are holy, 196 A Christmas Offertory, 226 In praise of Christ, 237 Praise Canon, 258 The Bridegroom's Song* and *262 Song of Farewell.*

Shaun MacCarthy, 43 Fallow Court Avenue, Finchley, London N12 0EA, for *223 Lamb of God* from *Mass of St George.*

Rev Christopher McCurry, English Martyrs Presbytery, St George's Road, Wallasey, Merseyside L45 6TU, for the music of *208 "Seventy Times Seven" Acclamations, 209 Responsorial Acclamations, 230 Ubi Caritas, 240 Entrance Antiphon and Procession of Palms, 251 Easter Vigil: Psalms and Alleluia* and *253 Easter Sequence.*

Riobard MacGorain, Gael-Linn, 26 Merrion Square, Dublin 2, Ireland, for *266 Ag Críost an síol / To Christ the seed* by Sean Ó Riada.

Rev Simon Peter McGrail, Christ the King Presbytery, 78 Queens Drive, Liverpool L15 6YG, for the music of *160 People of God, 210 Holy, holy, Memorial Acclamations A and B* and *Great Amen* and *224 Peace Song / Agnus Dei.*

Andrew Mackriell, 1 Portobello Harbour, Dublin 8, Ireland, for the music of *256 Psalm 32(33)* © Andrew J Mackriell 1990.

Make Way Music, PO Box 683, Hailsham, East Sussex BN27 4ZB, for *217 Peace to you* (1988) and *277 Shine, Jesus, shine* (1987) by Graham Kendrick © Make Way Music. International copyright secured. All rights reserved. Used by permission.

Mrs Josephine O'Carroll, c/o Kevin O'Carroll, Woodlands Ave, Halfway House, Co. Waterford, Ireland, for the music of *161 Entrance Psalm, 212 Memorial Acclamation, Great Amen* all from *Mass of the Annunciation,* Fintan O'Carroll © Mrs Josephine O'Carroll; *211 Holy, holy, 216 Our Father* all from *Mass of the Immaculate Conception,* Fintan O'Carroll © Mrs Josephine O'Carroll.

David Ogden, 41 Ralph Road, Horfield, Bristol BS7 9QR, for *166 White Light Kyrie* © David Ogden, Clifton Cathedral, Bristol BS8 3BX.

Chris O'Hara, 53 Pikes Lane, Glossop, Derbyshire SK14 8ED, for the music of *213 Carnival Sanctus* © Chris O'Hara 1990.

Peter Vaughan Ollis, Pine Heights, Old Neighbouring, Chalford, Stroud GL6 8AA, for *185 Alleluia.*

Geoffrey Phillips, 5 The Crescent, Adel, Leeds LS16 6AA, for *173 Festive Gloria* © Geoffrey Phillips.

Rt Rev Alan Rees OSB, Belmont Abbey, Hereford HR2 9RZ, for *186 Cardiff Papal Alleluia* and *239 Passion Sunday: Entrance Song* from *Lord by Your Cross* © Belmont Abbey Trustees.

Rev Ernest Sands, St Werburgh's Presbytery, St Werburgh's Square, Merseyside L41 2XZ, for the music of *267 May the choirs of angels* from *Order of Christian Funerals* (McCrimmons), © Ernest Sands 1988. Published by Oregon Catholic Press, 5536 NE Hassalo, Portland, OR 97213, USA. Administered in UK by Calamus, 30 North Terrace, Mildenhall, Suffolk IP28 7AB.

Bernard Sexton, 1 Kincora Drive, Clontarf, Dublin 3, Ireland, for *215 Eucharistic Acclamations 1: Holy, holy, Memorial Acclamation, Great Amen* and *236 Beannacht leat a Mhuire / Praise to God around us.*

Robert Sherlaw Johnson, Malton Croft, Woodlands Rise, Stonesfield, Oxon OX78 8PL, for the music of *164 No.1 of Chants for Penitential Rite 3* and *254 Easter Song: You sons and daughters of the Lord.*

Alan Smith, 7 Larchfield Close, Malvern Link, Worcs WR14 1RA, for the text and music of *165 Jesus, born for us* © Alan Smith 1991, and for the music of *237 Praise Canon* (reprinted by permission of Clifton Music) © Alan Smith 1992 and *241 Responsorial Psalm 21(22)* © Alan Smith 1992.

Taizé Community, for the music of *153 Prepare the Way* and *268 The Lord is my light* by Jacques Berthier © Ateliers et Presses de Taizé, 71250 Taizé Communauté, France.

Thankyou Music, St Anne's Road, Eastbourne, East Sussex BN21 3UN, for the music of *190 We believe* © 1986 Thankyou Music, *229 O Lord, Your tenderness* © Thankyou Music 1986, *260 Jesus, stand among us* © Thankyou Music 1977 and *276 God is good* © Thankyou Music 1985. All by Graham Kendrick, all used by permission.

Christopher Walker, 3745 Centilena Avenue 5, Los Angeles, CA 90006, USA, for the music of *187 Alleluia (Psalm 116(117)), 191 Creed: We believe, we believe, 231 Because the Lord is my shepherd, 244 Faith, Hope and Love (Mandatum)* and *250 Evening came and morning came.*

Rev James Walsh, The White House, 21 Upgate, Poringland, Norwich NR14 7SH, for *188 Gospel Acclamations: Praise to you, O Christ, Glory to you, O Christ* and *Glory and praise to you, O Christ.* Published by Oregon Catholic Press, 5536 NE Hassalo, Portland, OR 97213, USA. Administered in UK by Calamus, 30 North Terrace, Mildenhall, Suffolk IP28 7AB.

Andrew Wright, 44 Coram Green, Hutton, Brentwood, Essex CM13 1LW, for the music of *189 Advent Gospel Acclamations* © Andrew Wright 1992 and *199 The Grail Prayer* © Andrew Wright 1990, 1992.

Index of Composers and Authors

Please note that this index refers to the number of the item and not to the page.

Index of Titles and First Lines

RESPONSORIAL PSALM

Scriptural Index